SCHIZOPHRENIA: MEDICINE'S MYSTERY - SOCIETY'S SHAME

MARVIN ROSS

Dedicated to all who struggle daily with the voices and other symptoms of schizophrenia and to their families who suffer watching their loved ones valiantly struggling to cope

Table of Contents

PREFACE 5
INTRODUCTION 10
CHAPTER ONE – THE LACK OF PROGRESS IN THE CARE
AND TREATMENT OF SCHIZOPHRENIA 14
    The Mentally Ill in Jail 15
    The Mentally Ill on the Streets 20
    Report Card on Mental Health 22
    Treatment Outcomes 28
CHAPTER TWO – INDIVIDUAL EXAMPLES 33
    Some Successes 33
    The Slower Road To Recovery 36
    One Example of a Preventable Tragedy 40
CHAPTER THREE - A LEGACY OF IGNORANCE –
PHILOSOPHY FREUD AND NEUROBIOLOGY 50
    Introduction 50
    Schizophrenia Defined 55
    Physiological Deficits in Schizophrenia 59
    Studies on Non Treated Schizophrenics 62
        A. Structural Abnormalities 62
        B. Neurological Abnormalities 63
        C. Neuropsychological Abnormalities 66
        D. Electrophysiological Abnormalities 66
        E. Cerebral Metabolic Abnormalities 67
CHAPTER FOUR - THEORIES OF
CAUSATION/TREATMENT 73
    Genetics 73
    Infectious Agents 75
        Toxoplasma Gondii 76
        Other Viruses 78
    Marijuana 81
    Neurotransmitters – Cause or Chance Treatment Focus 82
    The Angel Dust/PCP Theory 85
    Other Neurotransmitters 94
    And Now some Controversy 94

CHAPTER FIVE – BEYOND CHLORPROMAZINE.............101
Deinstitutionalization 101
Anosognosia...107
Involuntary Treatment...108
Harvard Law School or Bellevue Psychiatric - Which is harder
to Get Into?..113
Involuntary Treatment Other Examples.......................117
CHAPTER SIX – TREATMENT STRATEGIES...................120
Consensus Guidelines 120
First Episode Early Intervention 123
Assertive Community Treatment (ACT).......................126
Mandated Outpatient Treatments (MOT) 128
Psychiatrists in Blue...131
A More Ideal System?...133
CHAPTER SEVEN – STIGMA 137
Introduction...137
In the Media 138
In the Military..140
A British Example...143
In the Medical Profession..145
CHAPTER EIGHT – THE NAYSAYERS..........................149
Scientology..149
The Consumer Survivor Movement..............................151
Alternative Medicine...156
CHAPTER NINE – CREATIVITY, MENTAL ILLNESS AND
FAMOUS PEOPLE WITH SCHIZOPHRENIA 159
AFTERWARD...163
REFERENCES...164
ALPHABETIC INDEX 173
ABOUT THE AUTHOR 185
ABOUT DAVID DAWSON 186

PREFACE

In 1968 I spent six months working as a psychiatric resident in a large mental hospital as part of a small group assigned by the University to develop a teaching ward. We unlocked the doors. We established community meetings. In keeping with the idealism of the times I refused to wear a white coat and carry keys. I talked with the patients. We tried our best to bring good medical and psychiatric care to ill people within a humanitarian environment.

But a large institution is a large institution. Acts of love, kindness, sympathy, and caring can be overwhelmed by bureaucratic indifference, collective needs, staff needs, budget considerations. And after midnight, when the University doctors had gone home, how do the orderlies manage unruly, sleepless, psychotic, sometimes aggressive men and crazy women? What does the night nurse have to do in order to report in the morning that they had an uneventful evening? In such institutions one can see both the very best and the very worst of human behavior.

And though they received three meals a day, could walk on the grounds they themselves mowed and raked, visit the Tuck shop, watch television in the lounge, attend occupational therapy classes and sleep in warm dormitory beds, almost all patients of these institutions, when asked, said they would prefer a place of their own, a home, no matter how poor it might be.

To the politicians these institutions appeared to cost a lot, especially when they housed people whose troubles, they suspected, were brought on by their own willful inadequacies. Denial of the reality of these illnesses was widespread then and now. Some even came to see the institutions, the mental hospitals, as causing mental disorder. And because these institutions were operated directly by province and state, the occasional scandal found its way to the legislature and the government. So politicians and governments would be happy to see them go, if possible.

Meanwhile idealistic doctors, nurses, psychologists and social workers, like myself, felt there must be a better way of helping people with mental illness. There were models elsewhere, some historical, some current and experimental. We had better, more effective medication now. North America was getting rich. We could develop community programs; the mentally ill could live in their own houses, or reasonable facsimiles thereof, and attend for treatment and counseling in their own communities.

Idealistic lawyers and civil libertarians, in keeping with the times, drew up new committal proceedings, building in hearings and appeal processes, and making "imminent danger to self or others" a necessary criteria for apprehension. And then they went further. As fundamentally illogical as it seems, they separated the rules for apprehending and keeping safely, from the rules governing involuntary treatment. The bar for capacity for consent to treatment was set very low. All of which meant, in practice, that a person could be and remain completely crazy, to his own and his family's serious (but not imminent) distress, vulnerability, and impairment and not fulfill the criteria for committal, and, some people, while deemed of such imminent danger to self or others as to warrant long term incarceration, might be found capable of consenting to treatment (which really means refusing treatment).

6

For a few years money was transferred from institutional budgets to community budgets; beds were closed at a pace aligned with the development of community programs, and low income supervised housing. The staff of that era enthusiastically pursued the ideal of delivering care to the mentally ill and their families in their communities. Some experimental models showed good results. But looking more carefully at those models I noticed that they usually relied on a single psychiatrist making home visits, being on call 24/7, on nurses taking people shopping, showing them how to cook, getting them up and dressed, spending long hours befriending and supporting, handing them medication. In reality it also meant we sometimes ignored the fine print of the Mental Health Act, took our syringes of anti-psychotic medication out to the boarding home, and persuaded our reluctant or ambivalent patients to bare their arms or drop their pants.

It didn't take long before the emptying of the mental hospitals outstripped the development of community resources, before the idealism of the staff waned, before less enthusiastic psychiatrists tired of the hours of preparation and presentation to review boards and committees required to get permission to treat obviously insane people, before they tired of appearing like, and feeling like fascists in the process.

As one psychiatrist put it succinctly, "the system allows us to distinguish between good patients (non-aggressive, compliant, cooperative) and bad patients." The "good" mentally ill patients get places to live, access to community treatment. The "bad" mentally ill patients are left to their own devices.

But as we know, organized communities will tolerate only so much disturbance, so much uncertainty. The shadowy, quiet homeless can be ignored, but not the man in your face, talking to himself, scaring customers away, stealing a loaf of bread, not paying cab fare. And so at a rapid pace, but quietly, two alternative institutions have grown to replace the old mental hospital: prisons and forensic psychiatry assessment facilities, both costing far more than the original mental hospitals, and neither more humane.

Cynically it must also be pointed out that these institutions (prisons, forensic services) provide work for battalions of lawyers.

Marvin Ross' commendable book is a survey of all this, examining what has happened in Europe, Canada, the USA, and Australia. As he writes, the mentally ill of many western countries are not faring as well as they might have in 1960 or 1970, despite our advances in knowledge, treatment, and our nations' wealth.

It is a depressing story. As one of those idealistic mental health professionals from the 1960's and 1970's, I feel the need to apologize. With the best of intentions we colluded with a revolution in the "delivery of mental health services". We didn't understand the pragmatics of politics. We didn't fully appreciate the community's need to deny the possibility of random brain-illness insanity. We didn't foresee the coming of Ronald Reagan and the neo-conservatives. We never guessed that in the year 2000 more people would believe in the devil, than in Freud, more people would believe in evil than frontal lobe impairment, and that Hollywood's version of mental illness would trump reality.

But as Marvin points out, some countries are doing a better job. Some have a more balanced approach. Some have found a better way of ensuring the mentally ill are afforded good medical treatment within a humanitarian environment, of not allowing (as one cynical psychiatrist once put it) "the seriously mentally ill to die in the back alleys with their rights intact."

David Dawson MD, FRCP(C)
Hamilton, Ont
March 2008

INTRODUCTION

S chizophrenia is an enigma. Far too often it completely destroys the lives of those it attacks along with the lives of their loved ones. It can also destroy lives of innocent bystanders and police. But, even though it's cause is not really understood and it's treatments are less than perfect, victims of this disease can be helped and they can lead better lives than many presently do.

Because the cause is not known or understood very well, it is a medical mystery. However, it is a disease that is very stigmatized. Many of its sufferers are condemned to living on the streets or in jail. It is also a disease about which so much misinformation is dispensed. Why else would so many people (and particularly those in the media and the entertainment world) feel that it is acceptable to belittle the sufferers of this disease and make fun of them or, worse, to portray them inaccurately and to demean them? That is society's shame.

It is bad enough to suffer from a debilitating chronic disease or to have a loved one who does but it is even worse to have to hide the existence of that problem from friends, family and strangers because of societal ignorance and stigma. And many do hide. Since gays have been able to leave the closet that they were forced to hide in for so many years due to ignorance and insensitivity, it has left more room in the closet for those with serious mental illness.

But, the point is that people with serious mental illnesses should not be treated like lepers and be forced to hide in the closet. It goes without saying that those with leprosy should never have been treated the way they were and we should not now treat those with schizophrenia in the same cruel and uncaring manner.

In her book, "Brave New Brain", noted psychiatrist Nancy Andreason says "losing a child by suicide may be the most painful experience a person can have. But observing how schizophrenia invades the personality and mental skills of an adolescent or young adult also causes nearly unbearable pain to both the young person and his family". And 10% of people with schizophrenia do commit suicide.

These victims of a biological illness should be able to hold their heads up and not be ashamed that they are ill. It is not their fault nor is it the fault of their families that they have a disorder of the brain. Their families, in fact, should be able to get support and sympathy from others for the pain that they suffer. Additionally, society should be protected from people who are capable of being a threat when not properly treated by ensuring that those in need of treatment do in fact get the treatment that they deserve and that will help them.

The purpose of this book is twofold. First, it is hoped that a candid discussion of the disease, the suffering that is inflicted on those with the disease by a mostly uncaring society and an explanation of what schizophrenia is and how the treatment of its victims can be improved will advance our appreciation of the problem. Second, it is intended that this book will provide information and comfort to the families of the victims and hopefully empower them in their struggle. It can also be used for families to give to friends and other family members in order to help them understand and to help to dispel the myths about serious mental illness they might have.

The last chapter provides information on well known people who have had or who have thought to have had schizophrenia. For some people, it provides comfort to know that many noted people or relatives of very noted people have suffered with schizophrenia. It certainly did for me and I hope that chapter and the rest of this book provide you with valuable information and help.

And now for a note on the terminology used in the book. Some people with schizophrenia and others with serious mental illnesses (and more so their politically correct advocates) do not like the reference to "schizophrenics". They feel that this marginalizes those people. They believe that calling someone a schizophrenic or a diabetic gives the impression that that person is only someone suffering from a disease and that they are not complete humans. Rather they are reduced to being a disease only.

In the mental health arena, the term that is preferred is consumer survivor and/or people with schizophrenia. Personally, I do not like these terms. Anyone who has been involved in the health system is a consumer of health care. If it did not kill you, then you are also a survivor. Consumer survivor is a term for those who feel that people with mental illnesses have either been improperly incarcerated in a totalitarian psychiatric system or diagnosed with a mental illness that might not exist. It differs from cancer survivor and is used like the phrase Holocaust survivor is used. The term implies that the individual has been unjustly imprisoned and possibly even tortured. It is a political concept that has dire consequences for getting people help and will be looked at in much greater length later in the book.

Calling someone a schizophrenic or a diabetic, on the other hand, does not necessarily demean them. It is an awkward style to continually use the phrase "people with schizophrenia" rather than simply saying "schizophrenics". While I vary the use of these two phrases for stylistic purposes, I do not do so to belittle.

The section of the book dealing with brain imaging is also a bit complex to say the least. Much of it may not be all that clear. The point is not to become an expert in the pathology of the brain but rather to get a feel for the fact that there are major changes that take place in the brains of people with schizophrenia that can be measured. It may be just in their heads but their heads are not normal.

Finally, a few people were kind enough to read the manuscript for errors and they did find some. However, any errors that still remain are the responsibility of the author.

CHAPTER ONE – THE LACK OF PROGRESS IN THE CARE AND TREATMENT OF SCHIZOPHRENIA

Today, replacing a defective heart with one from a recently deceased donor is commonplace and pretty routine. Plugged arteries that could lead to death are unplugged and kept open pretty much like the roto router man does with your toilet when it gets plugged up. Gallbladders and kidneys can be removed with keyhole surgery leaving only a couple of small scars, minimal pain and rapid recovery. Surgeons can even operate remotely via telerobotic surgery on someone hundreds of miles away.

Meanwhile, heart patients have a plethora of good drugs that will keep them alive for years. Infectious diseases like smallpox, polio and others have been eradicated or nearly so thanks to the development of vaccines. Infections have been tamed. Even HIV/AIDS which a mere 20 years ago was a sure death sentence has been relegated to a chronic condition.

What about schizophrenia - the most serious of the serious mental illnesses? It is a disease that afflicts one in one hundred of the population with no class or racial distinctions. It is a disease that strikes young people when they are just starting to become independent of their families. For males the onset is usually 18-25 and for females a bit older.

According to the World Health Organization, more that 50% of people with schizophrenia are not receiving appropriate care [1] Even in countries with well-organized health care systems, 44-70% of people with mental disorders receive no treatment at all. In a quarter of countries in the European Region, mental health services are not available in the community. [2] Some two million young people in the European Region of the World Health Organization suffer from mental disorders ranging from depression to schizophrenia and yet most of them receive no care or treatment. [3]

The Mentally Ill in Jail

We have regressed back to the early 1800s when it comes to our treatment of the mentally ill. As Judge Steve Leifman, an associate administrative judge in the eleventh judicial circuit court in Miami told "Time Magazine", "history is repeating itself. During the 1800s ..... families would simply drop their loved ones off at jails or prisons where their conditions remained untreated." [4]

The introduction to a symposium on mentally ill defendants in jail put on by the University of Miami School of Law at which Leifman was one of the participants, stated that "there are currently twice as many people housed in the jail who have mental illnesses than in the South Florida Evaluation and Treatment Center. On a daily basis, the jail holds between 800 and 1,200 inmates with serious mental illnesses." [5]

The document went on to say that these defendants are often held for committing petty crimes that could have been prevented if they had only received proper medical treatment. This lack of proper medical treatment often creates a "revolving door" for these inmates without ever solving their basic underlying medical problem and thus keeping them out of jail. [5,6]

In her book, "Crazy in America", which describes the experiences of six seriously mentally ill people with the prison system, Mary Beth Pfeiffer states that "here, in twenty-first century America, a prison system had recreated what America thought it had left behind: warehouses for the insane". [7]   She goes on to say that "they are dumping grounds for a difficult and growing population of mentally ill inmates".

L.A. police lieutenant Richard Wall is also quoted in the Time Magazine story pointing out that prisons have become the nation's de facto mental health care provider. There are currently 1.25 million inmates with severe diseases like schizophrenia "abandoned in the U.S. prison system instead of receiving treatment in hospitals." [4] Judge Leifman added "more Americans receive mental health treatment in prisons and jails than hospitals or treatment centers. In fact, the country's largest psychiatric facility isn't even a hospital. It's a prison – New York City's Rikers Island which holds an estimated 3,000 mentally ill inmates at any given time." [4]

The PBS show, "Frontline", did a program on the mentally ill in prisons called "The New Asylums" and provided data on the proportion of prisoners in each state diagnosed with mental illness and how much is spent for treatment for those prisoners. The data are available on the website at http://www.pbs.org/wgbh/pages/frontline/shows/asylums/etc/maptext.html

The best state is Arkansas where only 6% of their total prisoners had a mental illness in 2003. However, only 3% of the state's correctional budget was allocated to mental health. The correctional officials interviewed did not consider the 60 therapists on staff in 2004 to be an adequate number.

16

Vermont and Wyoming were the worst at 34.9% and 37.3% of prisoners who were ill with a mental illness.

One major reason for this situation that we will go into in greater detail later is that the number of hospital beds for psychiatric patients has drastically declined in the past few decades. Community resources needed to support these people in the community have not been established.

The analogy that can be made is that of closing all the residential beds for people who are mentally challenged (previously called mentally retarded), putting them out into the community and forcing them to fend for themselves without adequate housing, social support or professional care.

The Time Magazine article states that fifty years ago, the U.S. had nearly 600,000 state hospital beds for people suffering with mental illness but that has been decreased to 40,000 today.[4]   Judge Leifman, in testimony before a congressional committee in March, 2007 stated that the number of psychiatric hospital beds nationwide has decreased by more than 90% while the number of people with mental illnesses jailed and/or put in prison has grown by about 400%. "Some of the hospitals that were closed were actually converted into correctional facilities which now house a disproportionate number of inmates with mental illness". [6]

The California prison system advertises itself as one of the largest providers of mental health care in California [8 p.35] In 1995 an investigation in the California Corrections Department's treatment of mentally ill offenders by a federal judge cited a "rampant pattern of improper or inadequate care that nearly defies belief". [8 p.35] The report found that in one prison, mentally ill inmates were put into solitary confinement so frequently that it constituted "a deplorable and clearly conscious disregard for the serious mental health needs of inmates.....For those inmates, placing them in [solitary confinement] is the mental equivalent of putting an asthmatic in a place with little air to breathe" [7 p.35]

And yet, despite this gruesome picture, some families actually find that prison is the only place that they can get proper medical treatment for their loved ones. [8p.34] In other cases, police use "mercy bookings" for the mentally ill in order to protect them from potential violence that they may encounter on the streets. This is more often done for women for whom the danger of rape is a reality. [8 p.39]

According to Ken Braitmen, a co-ordinator with the National Alliance for the Mentally Ill (NAMI) in New Hampshire, "treatment has never been better for mental illness, but it has never been harder for those in need to get it. Funding shortages leave community mental health centers understaffed with underpaid workers who are buried beneath caseloads." As a result, many people wind up in jail. [9]

But the United States is not alone in its policies of deinstitutionalization and the consequences of putting sick people into jail.

In a 2005 report by Canada's correctional investigator, it was reported that the number of prisoners with mental illness had doubled over the previous 10-year period. [10] Between 1998 and 2004, the number of mentally ill prisoners increased by 50% while the total number of prisoners declined by about 12% [11] Support services for those prisoners lacked sufficient funding. [10]

18

Penny Marrett, the head of the Canadian Mental Health Association said "our prisons have become warehouses for the mentally ill due to funding cuts and closures in the community psychiatric facilities. This is an inhumane and unsafe way to address offenders with mental illness." .[11] Len Wall, the president of the Schizophrenia Society of Ontario said that "prison rules punish mentally ill prisoners for symptoms of their illness – such as being noisy or refusing orders." [11]

In Australia, over the past 20 years of planned closure of psychiatric beds, the number of patients in institutions has been more than halved from around 15,000 to 6,000. The prison population more than doubled between 1986 and 2001. There are more than 24,000 people in Australian prisons many of whom suffer from mental illness. In one study, 74% of prisoners in New South Wales (NSW) had a psychiatric disorder with almost 10% suffering symptoms of psychosis – the most serious of the psychiatric conditions. In another NSW study, it was found that 12% of prisoners are psychotic – a proportion that is 30 times the rate in the general population. [12]

An Australian Senate report stated that " [there are] serious concerns that, while the [psychiatric] institutions themselves have closed, institutionalization of people with mental illness has in fact been transferred to prisons and detention systems or been replaced with isolation within the community, for example, through homelessness". [12]

But, if jail is a barbaric manner for dealing with people who are sick, it is far better than being homeless. Ian Chovil, whose story will be recounted in chapter two, once commented that the first time he went to jail as a homeless person with undiagnosed and untreated schizophrenia, he thought he had gone on vacation. He had a semi private room (or cell), three meals a day and TV privileges.

The Mentally Ill on the Streets

The Treatment Advocacy Center of the Washington DC area, in its recent job ad for "a visionary leader" estimated that in addition to the estimated 300,000 people with acute psychiatric disorders in jails, there are an additional 200,000 poor souls out on the streets.[13] In his book, "Out of the Shadows", E. Fuller Torrey estimated that about 35% of the homeless suffer from severe mental illness. If we add in those with alcoholism and addictions, then the percent jumps to about 75% [8, p 17]

As with prison, one of the main reasons for this phenomenon is deinstitutionalization. In a study in Massachusetts, of 187 patients discharged from a public psychiatric hospital in 1983, 27% became homeless within 6 months. In Ohio, a similar study found that the proportion who became homeless was 35%. A 1995 study in New York put the figure at 38% [8, p 23]

Torrey describes as being the most ironic and poignant the the fact that shelters for the homeless were being established in buildings that were formally psychiatric institutions. Keener Men's Shelter in New York is an example. For 75 years, this building was part of the Manhattan State Hospital housing people ill with psychiatric disorders. As its beds emptied due to the deinstitutionalization policies, it was turned over to the City of New York who re-opened it in 1981 as a shelter for the homeless.

In 1990, it housed 800 homeless men of whom at least 40% were mentally ill. In fact, many of them had lived there when it was a hospital. One man with schizophrenia had lived in the shelter for seven years. Previously, he had lived in the same building when it was a hospital. The difference being that as a shelter it did not provide medical services to help him [8, p 23]

In the previous section, it was mentioned that often the police will arrest the homeless to protect them. Torrey cites studies on the occurrence of rape committed against homeless mentally ill women. One study of homeless women with schizophrenia found that 22% had been raped – two-thirds of them multiple times. A study in Baltimore put the rape figure at about one third and, in San Francisco, it was found that one poor woman was raped 17 times.

To protect themselves from attack, homeless women will often wear as many as 10 pairs of panty house at once and then add on numerous layers of clothing. [8 p 19-20]

Aside from rape and the potential to freeze to death, the homeless mentally ill are much more likely to get sick or die of other problems. One study in the UK that followed 48 homeless mentally ill people for 18 months found that three died in that period of time. One had an aortic aneurysm, one had a heart attack and one choked during an epileptic seizure. An additional three simply disappeared without taking their belongings with them. The mortality rate for this group was either 8% or 15% depending on how the missing three were classified (dead or just missing). [8, p 19]

More recently, it has been reported that in the UK, the percentage of people judged to be homeless with mental illness and/or disability rose from 3% in 1991 to 8% in 2006. [14]

A 2005-06 study conducted by the Canadian Institute for Health Information found that 52% of hospitalizations for the homeless were for psychiatric reasons. The rate of hospitalization for the rest of society was mainly for pregnancy and childbirth (13%). 35% of visits to the emergency by the homeless were for mental and behavioral disorders. This compares to 3% for the general population. The point is that there are significant numbers of mentally ill amongst the homeless in Canada. [15]

Nor is the situation any different in Australia. A church welfare group stated in 2005 that "homeless shelters are the community's de facto mental health institutions." More than 75% of the 847 people housed at the Wesley Mission's Edgar Eager Lodge in inner Sydney during that year had a mental illness or disorder. Of that group, 20% suffered from schizophrenia, 33% were bipolar and 26% had anxiety disorders. [16]

Interestingly, Switzerland allocates about 80% of its mental health budget to inpatient care compared to about 20% for other European countries. Only about 1.6% of those admitted for psychiatric care in Switzerland were homeless between 1998 and 2001. This compares to 20% for the UK and 35% for the US. [17] While not advocating that people with psychiatric diseases all be kept most of the time in institutions, these figures do suggest that discharging those with psychiatric illnesses to the community without proper supports goes a long way to account for the high incarceration and homeless rates being seen.

Report Card on Mental Health

As we saw in the previous two sections on jail and homelessness, the plight of those with serious mental illness is bleak. And yet, many governments continually put forth grandiose plans for improving the situation. The first president George Bush had this to say on July 17th, 1990 when he proclaimed the 90's to be the decade of the brain:

To enhance public awareness of the benefits to be derived from brain research, the Congress, by House Joint Resolution 174, has designated the decade beginning January 1, 1990, as the "Decade of the Brain" and has authorized and requested the President to issue a proclamation in observance of this occasion.

Now, therefore, I, George Bush, President of the United States of America, do hereby proclaim the decade beginning January 1, 1990, as the Decade of the Brain. I call upon all public officials and the people of the United States to observe that decade with appropriate programs, ceremonies, and activities. [18]

In 1999, the Surgeon General of the United States issued an immense report on mental illness in which it was stated:

The past 25 years have been marked by several discrete, defining trends in the mental health field. These have included:

1. The extraordinary pace and productivity of scientific research on the brain and behavior;
2. The introduction of a range of effective treatments for most mental disorders;
3. A dramatic transformation of our society's approaches to the organization and financing of mental health care; and
4. The emergence of powerful consumer and family movements. [19]

Then, in 2002, the second George Bush ordered another report to be done on mental health in the United States and:

"The President directed the Commission to identify policies that could be implemented by Federal, State and local governments to maximize the utility of existing resources, improve coordination of treatments and services, and promote successful community integration for adults with a serious mental illness and children with a serious emotional disturbance." [20]

Despite these three grandiose government commissions and proclamations, when the National Alliance on Mental Illness (NAMI) conducted the first comprehensive state-by-state analysis of mental health care systems done in 15 years, the results published in 2006 were far less than grandiose.

Every U.S. state was scored on 39 specific criteria and marks were given for infrastructure, information access, services and recovery supports.

This report confirmed what the Bush commission referred to above described as "a system in shambles" and what the Institute of Medicine of the National Academy of Sciences recently called a "chasm between promise and practice" [21]

Nationally, the overall grade for the United States was a D. Infrastructure and information access both received a D as well while services got a D+ and recovery supports received a C-.

Only five states received B's – the highest scores awarded. These were Connecticut, Maine, Ohio, South Carolina and Wisconsin. Seventeen states received C's, 19 states got D's and eight got F's.

The full report is online with details for every state but let us pick one of the best and one of the worst to see what they are doing or not doing as examples. Connecticut tied with Ohio with a straight B for the highest. Here is what Ohio is doing. There is:

- Strong state-level leadership in various branches of government
- Consumers and families play a prominent role in the system
- Impressive implementation of Evidence-based practices, decriminalization, and criminal diversion initiatives
- Productive dialogue between advocates and criminal justice system leaders

This state attained an A on information access.

However, they still have an urgent need to close gaps in funding, provide parity legislation and to address insufficient services. There are acute shortages of beds and staff. And Ohio is at the top of the heap.

Among the worst was the nearby state of Illinois which got a failing grade of an F. Their urgent mental health needs were:

- Balanced hospital and community service capacity
- Broad implementation of evidence-based practices
- Stronger collaboration to promote employment opportunities
- Jail diversion strategies, including re-entry programs

In summarizing the findings, NAMI medical director Ken Duckworth said "D's are unacceptable and C's cannot be considered a passing grade. If you need heart surgery, you don't want a surgeon who only got a C in medical school. The same principle applies in helping people with mental illness". [21]

Again, the United States is not unique. These failures exist in most of the developed and prosperous countries in the world.

In the Canadian province of Ontario, the government set up a task force "to focus on developing recommendations for regional and local improvements to mental health services across the province". Called "The Time is Now", 11 different reports were put together for ten regions and the province as a whole and were presented to the government in December 2002. [22]

The chair of one of the regional reports and the vice chair of the task force was Michael Wilson, a former senior member of the Canadian government whose own son had committed suicide. In a speech a few years after the reports were submitted to the Ontario government, Wilson said "only about 25% of those who need treatment actually get proper treatment. There would be a public outrage if these same statistics applied to those suffering with heart disease or cancer." [23]

The mental health system in Ontario, he said is not a system but "a hodge podge of ad hoc services that are fragmented, hard to understand, where the entry point was unclear, that was repetitive and a bewildering maze". He then added that mental health service was based "on 30 years of neglect that had led to staff shortages and little evidence based treatment."

Before the voluminous reports could be read, an election was called and the ruling party changed. Despite promises that some action would be taken by the new government, the reports languish somewhere. Wilson assured the audience that he and the other chairs would push for a response from the new government if one was not forthcoming. No response was forthcoming and Wilson has since been appointed to Washington as Canada's ambassador.

No fear though as the Canadian Senate jumped into the fray and conducted their own report. Called "Out of the Shadows at Last", this report with 118 recommendations was released in May of 2006. [24] It might be a bit too early to judge as it has only been about two years since the report was released but not much seems to have happened with the recommendations. However, in early 2008, the commission set out to try to develop a national action plan on mental health for Canada and to launch an anti-stigma campaign. Out of the Shadows, however is an interesting title. It was used by Fuller Torrey for his book in 1997 [8] and the problems he described are with us still.

Mental health services in the European Union are also quite varied. A 2004 report described services as being unequal and used suicide as an example. The rate per 100,000 of population ranged from a low of 3.6 in Greece to a world high 44 in Lithuania. As a consequence, the EU released a Green Paper entitled "Improving the mental health of the population: Towards a strategy on mental health for the European Union". [25]

In 2007, the Priory Hospital in England issued a report on the problems of stigma (to be discussed in a later chapter) and stated "mental illness is still shrouded in stigma, fear and ignorance". [26] The aim of the report is to raise awareness of the "shocking stigma" surrounding mental illness and in the way it affects treatment outcomes and employment options.

Up to this point, we have looked at global or societal indicators of the poor treatment provide by societies in the developed world. To use the current term "drilling down", we will devote the rest of this chapter to drilling down to look at how treatment actually impacts those treated. In the next chapter, we will go below that and examine some real cases.

Treatment Outcomes

And they are not very good. According to John McGrath, a professor at the Queensland Centre for Mental Health Research in Australia, "put simply, on average, patients with schizophrenia are two to three times more likely to die compared to the general population, and the gap is growing". He and his colleagues looked at 37 different studies from 1980 to 2006. All of these studies explored death rates among people with schizophrenia and covered 25 countries including the US.

Their results, published in the "Archives of General Psychiatry" in October 2007 found that the death rate for schizophrenics was about 2.5 times that of other people. The suicide rate was 13 times greater than the general population. Schizophrenics are also more likely to die of other major causes. This gap may widen in future as the newer medication used to control psychotic symptoms have side effects that increase weight, and make people more susceptible to type 2 diabetes and heart disease.

McGrath added that these data are a "tragic reflection on how suboptimal our current treatments are." [27]

In a recent article in the "Journal of the American Medical Association", Drs. John Newcomer of Washington University and Charles H Hennekens of Florida Atlantic University wrote that people with serious mental illness lose 25 years of life expectancy as compared with the general population. This loss is primarily due to an increased risk of cardiovascular disease. [28]

Mary V Seeman is a professor emeritus of psychiatry at the University of Toronto Faculty of Medicine. An internationally recognized researcher, she is in a good position to judge the progress (or lack thereof) of treatment for people with schizophrenia. She recently asked herself "are patients with schizophrenia better off in 2006 than they were when I started medical school 50 years ago?" [29] Her lengthy answer is provided in the "Canadian Journal of Psychiatry" and is worth looking at.

The answer, she said, probably depends upon what measures are used to determine successful outcome. In the 1950's a suitable or successful treatment was measured by how quiet the wards were. If noise was reduced and there was not too much burden placed on the nurses then treatment was successful. This led to the development of a supposed outcome measure called the Nurses' Observation Scale for Inpatient Evaluation that is still used today.

These institutions began to fill over the years and by 1946, in the US, nearly half the public hospital beds were occupied by people with mental illness. Because of overcrowding and inadequate staffing, deaths from infectious diseases like TB began to increase. Consequently, Dr. Seeman, states, a successful outcome for psychiatric patients became discharge into the community.

A positive outcome was seen as being able to discharge patients. A full evaluation of deinstitutionalization will be discussed later. However, what happened to these people was that they wound up in boarding homes or hostels "where optimal care was lacking". Patients returned to hospital often because they became unwell frequently.

Readmission rates became the measure of successful treatment. However, when people were evicted from these boarding homes and did not return to the hospital, they often ended up in the street. Hungry and poor, they often committed petty crimes like shoplifting and ended up in jail.

Dr. Seeman refers to a recent study in San Francisco where nearly three quarters of a sample of severely mentally ill people had been arrested at some point.

None of the above treatment outcome measures that have been used over the past 50 years include wellness on the part of the sick person. Have they been quiet? Could we discharge them from hospital? Did they not come back? They might have been sick and unable to cope but if they were quiet, could be discharged and did not find their way back then the system had done a good job.

Professor Seeman then goes on to look at the general health of people with schizophrenia in 2006. In her words, it "is far from good. Rates of obesity, smoking, angina and respiratory symptoms are significantly higher than in the general population". In one study, it was found that the 10-year risk of cardiovascular disease was significantly elevated in subjects treated for schizophrenia as compared with age-matched control subjects.

30

Schizophrenia patients had significantly higher rates of smoking (68% vs 35%), diabetes (13% vs 3%), hypertension (27% vs 17%), and high cholesterol (percentages not given). Additionally, mortality is higher for schizophrenics for most diseases along with suicide and causes of unknown origin. Anywhere from 16-25% of schizophrenics are victims of violence. A British study found that men with schizophrenia have an increased risk of dying by homicide especially when they are involved in alcohol and drug use. Suicide rates are also high at about 10 to 20 times the rate of the general population.

The only bright spot in all this is that for some reason, people with schizophrenia are not more likely to develop cancer. Only one study showed higher rates while all others have shown the rate to be the same.

The bottom line from the above is that the life expectancy of people with schizophrenia is 20% lower than for the general population. Average life expectancy in the US is 76 years (72 for men and 80 for women) but only 61 for schizophrenics (57 for men and 65 for women).

Part of the cause of increased cardiovascular diseases, weight gain and diabetes is treatment. Numerous studies have found associations between treatment with antipsychotic drugs and the markers for developing these diseases. Dr. Seeman summarizes them stating "antipsychotics are a significant factor for sudden cardiac death".

There may not be much choice in the drugs that are used when balancing active psychosis versus sanity and an increased risk of other diseases but better social supports would help. Dr. Seeman states that most people with schizophrenia are more or less on their own battling a serious health problem with insufficient support. She wonders if some of this might not be the "direct result of professional negligence".

In addition to better medication, she concludes, we could probably use a system of foster families to look after vulnerable individuals as is common in Europe.

The problems of deinstitutionalization and better supports for these people who are ill will be discussed in much greater detail in later chapters.

CHAPTER TWO – INDIVIDUAL EXAMPLES

I t is time to put a face to all the statistics that were bandied about in the previous chapter. We are, after all, talking about real people with loved ones who care about them. It should also be pointed out that all is not gloom and doom. There are positive outcomes and there could be even more positive outcomes if we provided proper care and treatment for the ill amongst us.

Regrettably, we rarely learn of the successes because those who have conquered this illness, learn to deal with it as well as they can and those who have done well, rarely admit it. Many of them remain in that metaphorical closet once inhabited by themselves and the gay community. Gays have, for the most part, left the closet but thanks to the stigma surrounding mental illness, many sick people still hide in there. While they at least have more room, the point is that they should not be in the closet at all. They should be able to receive proper care and treatment and they and their families should be able to hold their heads up in public and not be scorned.

Some Successes

Elyn Saks is a college valedictorian, an Oxford scholar, a Yale law school graduate and a professor of law at the University of Southern California. She is also a schizophrenic who hid her affliction for many years before finally "coming clean" with her 2007 book "The Center Cannot Hold: My Journey Through Madness".

In September 2007, she spoke to the American

Psychological Association meeting in San Francisco. In its description of her presentation, the LA Times stated very eloquently that for "over 30 years, as she forged her career, she wrestled with uncouth visions, violent commands and suicidal impulses. Saks explained to her listeners in her worst moments the TV made fun of her, ashtrays danced and walls collapsed. Sure she was a witch, she burned herself as punishment with cigarettes, lighters and electric heaters. She believed she was single-handedly responsible for the deaths of thousands of people. The brains of close associates were taken over by aliens." [30]

Despite being hospitalized while at Oxford, Saks graduated in 1981 with help from antipsychotic medication. It controlled the symptoms and allowed her to hide her illness from those around her. She was later hospitalized again while at Yale Law School until her newly emerged symptoms could be controlled with an increase in medications. During her stay in hospital, she spent time reading her law books in the ward day room. When she was discharged and returned to her studies, she began to focus on the complex topic of civil issues in mental health law and represented psychiatric patients charged with crimes.

Researching a paper on the use of restraints on psychiatric wards, she mentioned to a professor how such devices could be both frightening and demeaning to patients. The response she got was "you don't really understand, these people are different than you and me. It doesn't affect them the way it would affect us".

Imagine saying that about African Americans. No need to treat their pain the same way we do white folks because they do not experience pain the way we do.

Saks contrasted getting breast cancer with developing schizophrenia since she also developed that malady in 1999. Friends and colleagues sent her flowers when they learned of her illness but, she commented, when you lose your mind, no one sends you get well flowers or offers sympathy of any sort.

An even more blatant example of why victims of psychiatric diseases hide in the closet was the comment that Ms Saks got when she came out of the closet. One USC staff person told her after she outed herself that "she would never have gone to dinner with her had she known of her schizophrenia afraid that one of her delusional episodes could occur at any time."

Not only do people with serious mental illnesses have to endure a chronic illness with only minimal symptom control, they and their families must live in fear of others finding out about their "shame". They are denied the support and encouragement that we give to those with other chronic illnesses like AIDS, cancer, Alzheimer's, etc.

The burden of the psychiatric patient is multiplied and the pain intensified.

Fred Frese is a successful psychologist and a member of the board of NAMI. He too is schizophrenic with a history of involuntary hospitalizations in various military, state, county, Veterans, and private hospitals in Florida, Alabama, Maryland, Wisconsin, Texas, and in Ohio, where he was judicially determined to be an insane person and committed to the local public psychiatric hospital in the summer of 1968.

Although his court commitment occurred over 35 years ago, Fred has yet to receive official notification that he has been restored to sanity. He is sure this must be an oversight. He has not been re-hospitalized since 1976 but in a workshop he conducted in Hamilton, Ontario a few years ago, he said that he still has periodic breakdowns and he also still has delusions that "certain high ranking US officials are not behaving as they should but", he said, "increasingly other Americans are beginning to share that delusion".

His delusions might be a bit prophetic because he made that statement at a workshop attended by this author who wrote about it back in 1999.

The interesting part of Frese's history is that he became paranoid and delusional while a young captain in the US Marines. He was a guard at one of the largest repositories of nuclear weapons in the US with 144 well-armed marines under his command. He was convinced that his superior officers had been hypnotized by the enemy and that the bombs were in danger. His delusion was so strong that it resembled a religious belief.

Despite his illness and his hospitalizations, he did manage to get a PhD in psychology in 1978 and then go on to become director of psychology at Western Reserve Psychiatric Hospital in Ohio. He also picked up a business degree along the way. [31,32]

The Slower Road To Recovery

Both Elyn Saks and Fred Frese were medically treated early and probably with all the latest resources that modern psychiatry has to offer. They were both able to go on and become successful in their lives as many people are able to do. For some people, the process is much slower as there is often a reluctance to diagnose schizophrenia, it is just simply missed as a possible diagnosis, patients are reluctant to take medications, or they do take them and get a bad reaction.

The importance of early intervention and the need for more programs will be discussed later in this book. An important point to note is that like many diseases the longer it remains undiagnosed and untreated the greater the brain damage. "Once the damage is done, it cannot be undone. Neither love nor money can ever undo the damage of delayed treatment for schizophrenia. The individual is disabled for the rest of his or her life."

These words were spoken by Ian Chovil who was quoted earlier in this book. His own diagnosis and treatment was delayed for over ten years. His life today would have been considerably different if he had been treated early. In addition to the human cost, the cost to society would have been much less with early diagnosis and treatment.

He went on to say that "it is only too self evident to me that I have permanent damage that I must live with because I was not treated in the first six months. It is something that I think about everyday, something I have to re-accept every morning". [33]

Today, Ian is retired from a job that he had at an internationally renowned psychiatric, behavioral and addiction treatment facility called the Homewood Health Centre in Guelph Ontario but he continues to update his excellent website on schizophrenia (chovil.org).

From the introduction to that site he said "I have schizophrenia and have been on medication now since 1990, the length of time I have lived in Guelph. I'm 53 and I have had schizophrenia for the last 36 years. That includes about 8 years of prodromal symptoms, 12 years of untreated psychosis, and 17 years of treatment with antipsychotics. Between 1980 and 1990, I was experiencing a very disabling psychosis, alone and very poor. I eventually got in trouble with the law in 1988 and received three years probation with the condition that I see a psychiatrist for those three years. I've been to jail, been actively alcoholic, attempted suicide, and was homeless for six months in 1980." [34]

How Ian got to court is a fairly typical story. The son of a physician, he did very well in school and at the age of 16 scored in the top three percentile in a mathematics contest in the entire province of Ontario. By the age of 18, he began losing interest in his friends and began drinking and using marijuana - a not untypical scenario. The use of alcohol and marijuana is considered to be a form of self medication for the subtle symptoms and feelings of unease that precede a full blown case of schizophrenia.

Because of family pressures, Ian went to university and graduated with an honors BSc in biology and anthropology. He then went on to graduate school in Nova Scotia but often visited the student health office. He thought the water supply was contaminated and that he might die of a heart attack. His delusions got worse and he became convinced that he was being poisoned with dioxin and that he had a form of syphilis that could not be detected by blood tests.

He was referred to a psychiatrist who prescribed antipsychotic medication. Shortly after, he was hospitalized for a couple of weeks. He continued his decline after his discharge and this time he was hospitalized involuntarily. After treatment with more antipsychotic drugs, his delusions ceased, his mind cleared and he was discharged again. He was encouraged to continue taking his medication but was never told why that was necessary or how long he should continue.

Schizophrenia and psychosis were never mentioned to him or to his father – a doctor.

Ian left school and his medications behind and went off to the west coast where he again lapsed into a full fledged psychotic state. He became homeless but did visit numerous family physicians about his physical complaints and fear of dioxin poisoning. No one ever suggested schizophrenia to him.

In 1985, he was homeless in Toronto living in his car when he was charged by the police with mischief and carrying a concealed weapon. Convicted, he was sentenced to three years probation and ordered to see a psychiatrist as part of his probation. He completed the sentence in the nearby city of Guelph and has been well since.

In his website biography, Ian said "the quality of my life has been improving a little each year for the last fourteen years and I can't complain too much but every once in awhile I really feel the losses I am enduring. Life is a series of opportunities as you grow older, and I missed every one. It is only in the past couple of years that I can say that I have been able to accomplish anything productive. Before that I was pretty unhappy and didn't feel very good about myself".

Ian is lucky. At least he was eventually diagnosed and treated and was able to resume his life and be productive although at a late age. He is not alone. So many people with schizophrenia are not diagnosed and/or are not treated appropriately thus wasting what could be very productive lives, causing pain and heartache to their families and costing society wasted dollars.

The next section will deal with an extreme example of what can happen when a proper diagnosis is not made and the victims of this disease are not treated. What you are about to read is unfortunately not that rare an event and is what Dr. Torrey refers to as "preventable tragedies".

One Example of a Preventable Tragedy

This is the story about a woman and her brother and I am going to report it as she told it with some minor editing and the removal of hospital names. I have been asked not to use personal identifiers in order to respect the privacy of the family and because the ill person "is recovering and may have a shot at life after all that has happened. He is already worried about his privacy as he hopes to eventually work again". Here is their story: [35]

Looking back, I can now see that there were signs that something was wrong with my brother Richard around 1998. These were very subtle changes. At first my parents and I thought he was dealing with depression. He was about 22 at the time and about to enter his fourth year of university. That summer he was excited about school and was talking about doing graduate work. At Thanksgiving he came home and told my parents he wasn't going back, end of story. At the time they didn't push him for answers - they told him they didn't agree, but it was his decision.

He started working and everything seemed fine and he was saving money for a trip - backpacking to Mexico and Central America.

He still seemed fine, but had started to push away some friends. By the way, all the way through school Richard always had throngs of friends. He was handsome, charming, athletic and popular. Now, he wasn't as interested in doing the things he would normally do. By 2000, he had really retreated from his friends, only seeing a few of them. As well, Richard's 'social' marijuana habit became a regular habit. (Of course my parents did not approve, but pot is labeled a soft drug and I guess they didn't know what to do). I'm sure if they could have seen into the future they would have tried harder to get him to stop his marijuana use, but even they knew people who had successful lives who were regular users. So I guess they didn't think too much of it.

Richard left for his trip in March of 2001. At that time he was still fine but he had become a bit eccentric. He returned in May of that year having run out of money. He was quiet upon his return but seemed at peace with things. He decided to go back to school for the summer session to finish his degree.

He was there maybe about three weeks when my dad had to pick him up as he became very sick with malaria. It took him about a year to recover from that. My parents told him to not worry about school or work and that he should focus on his health.

At the end of 2001, we began to see his paranoia and began to hear some very scary things coming out of him. I think the three of us were in shock at first. At one point he told me the police in Mexico had followed him to the airport to make sure he left the country.

By mid 2002 it was obvious something was very wrong and we began to try to get him to see a doctor. One of the tricky

41

things too about Richard is he would come in and out of this state. He would be a stranger one-minute and then he would be the 'old' Richard (is how we described it) the next. It was a confusing time and we didn't know what we were dealing with.

By this time Richard was talking about his thoughts being stolen and that he was receiving messages from the TV.

In January of 2003 my parents went to a Schizophrenia education clinic. They definitely felt that Richard had a lot of symptoms of schizophrenia but there were some symptoms that he did not have. Later on, when he was finally assessed properly, I was told he did not present as a textbook case.

Richard was very high functioning and was always very clean about himself - obsessively sometimes. After the education program was over my parents told my brother where they had been. He freaked out and told them he wasn't crazy but they were and to prove it he would see the social worker who had conducted the program.

BIG MISTAKE!!!!!!!

He went and of course he knew to pull himself together. The social worker met with him for about 45 minutes. She later informed my father that Richard didn't have schizophrenia but that he had bad behavior and all he needed to do was get a job.

We were floored and thought we were the crazy ones after all. We then thought all of the problems he had were because of the drugs.

Richard got worse. He became very mean. He became prejudiced and racist against everyone. In fact he was very upset that I had given birth to my daughter at a Jewish hospital and now my baby was starting her life off tainted. My husband is from a catholic background and he was also targeted as being evil. When we baptized our daughter he told me I was horrible for doing this to her. So his obsession with religion became very disturbing. He joined the Mormons and had become very involved in aboriginal traditions before this.

After the social worker told us he didn't have a mental illness, we probably lost a year in getting him help. A professional had told us we were wrong and we were just going in circles. Finally at the beginning of 2004 we began to think again that this was not just a drug problem. We tried everything to get him to go to see a doctor. He was paranoid of course and claimed all doctors were evil and out to take his 'energy'.

I called the first episode clinic and briefly spoke to a nurse and then had my dad call there. He spoke to the same nurse as well as a doctor (I'm assuming a psychiatrist). She told dad that Richard was someone they definitely wanted to see but they needed a referral from a family doctor (GP). At that time, Richard didn't have a GP. The one he had growing up had left the country. Dad asked his own GP to do a blind referral to the clinic but the doctor refused.

Then dad asked him to refer himself and my Mom to someone who could help them deal with their son. The doctor said "What for?" I guess he thought my parents didn't know what they were talking about. I still get angry when I think about this person and him not helping or at least trying to help.

Mom and dad then went to see a 'therapist' through my mother's employee program. She of course was totally inexperienced in mental health issues (at least at this level) and told them they were great parents for sticking by their son.

That was May of 2004.

So there we were. We had asked for help and kept going in circles. I know my parents were exhausted. At this point they were really living with a terrorist in their home. He watched my mom cook, because he thought she was poisoning him. He followed them around to listen to what they had to say. He was very paranoid and then came the physical aggression.

I think it was in May of that year that he was angry with my dad for something. He pushed dad against a wall and held him by the collar. Screaming at him about whatever the problem was. He also put his hands around dad's throat and threatened him.

At this point we started to talk about having him charged in order to get him help. Though at that time we didn't know about court diversion programs. As well, we talked about getting him into the hospital involuntarily.

In August things became worse and Richard began to accuse my father of having sex with my daughter. My dad was very upset. I think he could take all of the abuse from my brother but when he brought my daughter into it (who wasn't even two) it was just too much. But things calmed down again.

In September, he attacked my father again. This time leaving bruises on my father's neck. I can't believe we didn't *have him charged then, but of course my parents were afraid of Richard going to jail and getting lost in the system rather than getting help.*

Desperate, we begged Richard to go to the hospital. I even tried to reach him from the angle of his drug use. It seemed easier than saying we think you have a mental illness.

On the Thanksgiving weekend my parents told my brother he was able to live with them and they would take care of him but they would not be giving him money because they knew he used it for drugs. He was stealing money from them and would take their cards whenever he liked.

An outsider looking in would probably think my parents should have been tougher earlier, but I think everything just spiraled before they knew what happened. And if you have lived with someone with a serious mental illness you know how this can happen.

Well, that Thanksgiving was pretty awful. On the Saturday, my dad called the police to ask them if they could come to take Richard to a hospital. The police told him to call the courthouse and he should try to get a judge to sign a form to have him taken to the hospital. The phone number my dad was given had a recording saying the courthouse was closed for the weekend. Dad called back the same officer - I'm not sure what was said but my dad was very upset. So he decided he would call the courthouse the next Tuesday. By the way, I later found out there is always a JP at the courthouse on Saturdays for bail court. If we had gone in person, we might have received some help.

My parents stayed at my house on the Saturday night and it was a lovely peaceful evening.

On Monday, Richard said he wanted the car for the next day to look for a job. That was fine because dad wanted Richard out of the house to make his calls to the courthouse. Dad worked from home.

On the Tuesday, mom left work and my dad ran some errands. When he came home, I later found out, that my brother attacked him with a hammer. Richard then strangled him to make sure he was dead. The autopsy said he died of blunt force trauma to the head, with asphyxiation being a death factor. Richard took off my father's clothes and inspected his body. He wrapped him up in a tarp and put his body in the basement behind some drywall. He cleaned up the mess. He then ran some errands, took money out of my parents account.

Eventually Richard ended up at my house and as luck/chance would have it, my husband happened to be home. He wasn't supposed to be. Richard talked to us for a bit. We later found out he had brought a hunting knife with him. Presumably he was going to kill my daughter and I, although he denied this. He then went home and waited for mom. (During this time, mom and I we were calling dad and we had even thought of calling the police but thought we were over- reacting.)

When mom returned home I spoke to her on the phone at about 4:25pm. She then called her sister. She told me dad wasn't home (Richard made up a lie about him going out with a colleague) and Richard wasn't upstairs in the office. Mom then went up to the washroom. Apparently when she was washing her hands Richard burst in on her and attacked her with a hunting knife. He went for her throat and missed, cutting her deeply in the face and on her hand. He then was able to overpower her and he cut her throat, so much so she was almost decapitated. There were other stab wounds, but these were apparently post-mortem.

Richard then wrapped her up in a blanket and put her beside my father. He cleaned up again. He cut himself during the attack and went to the hospital for stitches. It was too long of a wait so he went to the police station and asked to speak to an officer. He told the officer that he had found two dead bodies at his house and they should check it out. Of course they found my parents and later charged Richard with two counts of first-degree murder.

Richard was later diagnosed with paranoid schizophrenia, having misidentification delusional disorder or Capgras Syndrome. It turns out he thought my parents had been stolen and taken over by imposters. This is why he had inspected my father's body. He later claimed that 'the man's' body was distorted. He also removed a necklace from my mother's neck and commented that he thought it was weird that this woman would have something on that belonged to my mother. As well, he thought all of his friends and family were slowly disappearing.

He later told me that he thought mom and dad were going to show up and set everything straight. Richard even thought if DNA testing were done the courts would acquit him because these people weren't his parents.

He spent 11 months in jail and finally after assessments and court proceedings Richard was found to be not competent due to a mental disorder. He has been in a medium security psychiatric facility for almost a year. And he is doing very well. He has been on antipyschotic medication since late April 2005 and it has worked very well for him. I know that my brother was/is ill. And I support his rehabilitation. It is only in the last couple of months that I *have noticed that he is actually processing what he has done. Before, his team told me that he had intellectualized everything. Now I see the pain in his eyes.*

Unfortunately, I am the only family member who is supporting him. My parent's siblings have, for the most part, refused to see this for what it is. If they really cared for their siblings they would know that they would be thrilled that their son was finally getting help. They died trying to get him help.

Looking back, I can see all of the mistakes we made. I know so much now and of course I wish I had known it then. The first forensic psychiatrist who assessed Richard told me that even if we had been able to get him in for assessment prior to my parents deaths, that he would have been released because he was very good at hiding his illness.

When my parents died, I made a promise to them that I would work the rest of my life to make changes to the mental health system.

Horrendous as this story is, it is not all that unique. One lesson that should be learned from this emphasized by his sister is that once he began treatment in jail, he "responded immediately to the first med they tried and all of his symptoms have dissipated". For an up to date list of preventable tragedies and/or to see what happens in your own state if in the US, see Fuller Torrey's website at http://www.treatmentadvocacycenter.org/ep.asp.

People with untreated mental illness sometimes kill, commit suicide and are killed by others but none of the pain, the heartache and the wasted lives has to happen. Much of it can be prevented. If only people understood that this is an illness of the brain and not a character flaw then they might (should) demand treatment. Hopefully, the rest of this book will demonstrate to readers what schizophrenia is and how our treatment can be improved.

CHAPTER THREE - A LEGACY OF IGNORANCE – PHILOSOPHY FREUD AND NEUROBIOLOGY

Introduction

Since man first began to walk the earth, he sought out explanations for what he saw around him and within himself. Concepts about the heart, blood and circulatory system are an example. The Greeks believed that the heart was the seat of the spirit, the Egyptians believed it was the center of the emotions and the intellect, while the Chinese believed the heart was the center for happiness.

Galen, a Greek physician who spent years studying blood, believed and taught his students that there were two distinct types of blood. 'Nutritive blood' was thought to be made in the liver and was then carried through veins to the organs, where it was consumed. 'Vital blood' was thought made in the heart and then pumped through arteries to carry the "vital spirits." Galen further believed that the heart acted not to pump blood, but to suck it in from the veins. He also believed that blood flowed through the septum of the heart from one ventricle to the other through a system of tiny pores. He did not know that the blood left each ventricle through arteries.

Thanks to the English physician, Harvey, and the work that has progressed from that point, science has a much better understanding of how the heart and the circulatory system really work. Because of that knowledge, modern medicine can interfere surgically to repair heart damage and has developed drugs to partly reverse heart pathologies that lead to damage and death.

Our understanding of how the brain works is not that advanced. In fact, is it the brain or is it the mind? The brain is a physical organ that you can hold in your hands but what is the mind? It is an abstract concept and, going as far back as Plato, the mind and the body were seen as two distinct entities. The French philosopher Descartes further advanced this concept of a mind-body split (dualism). The mind was seen as a separate entity from the body and it was non-physical. If the mind was non-physical then the laws of biology would not apply.

According to psychiatrist Nancy Andreason, the distinction between mind and brain is embedded in the language we use everyday. Brain, she says, refers to a physical organ while mind refers to an abstract concept. Because it is not palpable, the mind is sometimes considered less real [36]. However, mind and brain are two different words that refer to the same thing or activity. Neither can exist without the other.

The link between mind and brain, she says, has been around since Neolithic times. Skulls have survived with holes drilled into them (trephined) which was a medical treatment done to let out the evil spirits. These evil spirits were believed to cause mental illness and epilepsy.

The false dichotomy between mind and brain can be and is used to misunderstand and mistreat people. Dividing illness into physical/neurological versus mental results in the former group of illnesses being treated with respect while the latter – the mental – being stigmatized.

Early medical texts going back as far as 1900 BC and to the Egyptian Ebers Papyrus and the writings of Hippocrates and Galen described mental illnesses. They are described in the Bible as, Dr. Andreason points out, Saul suffered depression. In all these early medical texts, mental disorders were considered the same as physical illnesses. The organ affected was the brain.

All this changed about the 1500s. Between the fall of the Roman Empire and the scientific and philosophical revolution of the 17th century, the church held most of the power, wealth and influence. Deviations in belief were not tolerated. Those poor souls who did deviate from accepted belief were deemed to be possessed and books were written to describe how to identify these witches and those others possessed by the devil. "Malleus Maleficarum" or "Hammer of Witches" was one such text written by two Dominican monks. Much of what they described were symptoms of what doctors today would diagnose as psychotic depression and schizophrenia.

A similar tome was written by the Protestant King of England and Scotland, James I. He published his book "Demonologie" in 1611 and it was similar to the Catholic text.

Fortunately, in the late 1800s, scientists were beginning to look at the physiology of the brain just like their colleagues were looking at the physiology of the rest of the body. Unfortunately, this effort was derailed by the Freudians whose influence set neurobiology back decades and whose influence is still being felt today.

Fuller Torrey points out in his book that in the late 18th century both psychiatrists and neurologists were beginning to see that insanity was a disease of the brain. In fact, at that time, John P Gray, president of what was to become the American Psychiatric Association had pathologists examine the brains of those with mental illness in the asylum that he headed.

Torrey goes on to say that this emphasis on the physical as a cause of mental illness changed in 1909 first with the founding of the National Committee for Mental Hygiene and then, later that year, with the visit of Sigmund Freud to the US. This organization was modeled after similar groups whose goal was to prevent conditions like TB and infant mortality. The mental hygiene group was originally intended to reform mental hospitals but it quickly became a movement to promote mental hygiene and it aligned itself with the ideas of Freud.

It also soon aligned itself with the social and liberal reform movements that were growing at the same time. It quickly adopted the belief that "mental disorders tend to thrive on the soil of faulty habits and unsatisfactory environments". [8] p149 Within 10 years, according to Torrey, this group had been completely taken over by those who followed Freud and the social reformers.

By the 1920s, the mental hygiene movement hooked up with the child guidance advocates. Juvenile delinquency was a problem and they thought that Freudian child rearing techniques could prevent delinquency and mental disorders. The influence of these ideas continued into the 1930s and mental hygiene and Freudian psychoanalysis became even more closely associated with liberal ideas. With the spread of Hitler in Europe, many Jewish analysts who were also left leaning fled to the US and influenced the New York intelligentsia.

Torrey states that Freud himself never really understood why his ideas had become so attractive to the American social reformers and liberals. Freud was conservative, opposed the Russian revolution and supported the reforms of Benito Mussolini. Nonetheless, by the time of Freud's death, mental illness was seen as resulting from childhood experiences and social circumstances. Prevention required intervention at an early age in order to prevent those negative circumstances from producing a mentally ill individual.

As for serious mental diseases like schizophrenia, that was considered to be the cause of poor mothering. In fact, some psychiatrists came up with the term "schizophrenogenic" mothers or parents to describe dysfunctions within the family that could produce this disorder. As Abram Hoffer put it in his memoirs, by the 1950s "many psychoanalysts proclaimed that schizophrenia was not a disease. They saw it as a reaction, a way of life, induced by intrapsychic conflicts or by conflicts with authority figures (usually the mother)" [37]

Hoffer was, and still is, a very controversial figure in schizophrenia research partly, this author suspects, because whether he was right or wrong, he was ahead of his time. He looked for biological causes when the Freudians were in charge. More will be said of him later.

In the 1960s and into the 70s (and even today), an anti-psychiatry movement grew up fueled by people like Thomas Szasz and R. D. Laing. Szasz was the author of a highly popular book called "The Myth of Mental Illness". He argued that people are not ill but that they are defined as ill because they hold ideas that are not popular. Szasz titled one of his books "Schizophrenia: The Sacred Symbol of Psychiatry". Laing was a Scottish psychiatrist who believed that schizophrenic symptoms are a reaction to the impossible demands that are put on people and particularly impossible demands from their own family. These views became popular, in part, because of the "beatnik/hippie" social climate of the time and because of the excesses of psychiatry in dictatorships like that of the Soviet Union.

Research into the biological causes of schizophrenia and other serious mental disorders was stonewalled by the emphasis of the social reformers, the psychoanalysts and the anti-psychiatrists. We are still not quite over that but progress is being made. However, that is not to say that environment and child rearing practices do not have some influence on people. They do and some of it may be good while some of it may be bad.

Schizophrenia Defined

It is a disease that is very much misunderstood and therefore often feared and/or belittled, trivialized and even demonized. Many perceive of it as a split personality – a Dr. Jeckell and Mr. Hyde syndrome. The word schizophrenia was coined by the Swiss psychiatrist, Eugen Bleuler in 1908 and was meant to describe the separation of function between personality, thinking, memory and perception.

The word schizophrenia is from the Greek roots schizein (split) and phren (mind). The split was meant to describe a split from function or an incongruence between mood or affect and words, but it soon began to take on the meaning of split or dual personality. Because of this misconception, the Japanese term for schizophrenia was changed in 2004 from Seishin-Bunretsu-Byo (mind-split-disease) to Tōgō-shitchō-shō (integration disorder). In 2006, campaigners in the UK, under the banner of Campaign for Abolition of the

Schizophrenia Label, argued for a similar rejection of the diagnosis of schizophrenia and a different approach to the treatment and understanding of the symptoms currently associated with it.

It is estimated that about one person out of 100 has the disease that usually starts in late adolescence. At least, the more overt and noticeable symptoms begin roughly from about the age of 18 to 25. It is now believed that more subtle symptoms of the disease – called the prodrome – begin earlier.

Prodromal symptoms refer to the beginning or precursor symptoms of an illness. It refers to the "at risk" stage of psychosis, when an individual is experiencing mild symptoms, but is not yet psychotic. [38] People who suffer migraines are familiar with this concept. In that disease, prodrome refers to the sometimes vague symptoms experienced by an individual before there is a full blown painful symptomatic migraine.

Individuals who are at risk for developing a psychotic illness usually experience mental and emotional changes before more serious symptoms develop. These early signs of risk are often non-specific, sometimes even barely noticeable. An unexpected decline in a person's usual way of functioning or relating to others may be an indicator that she/he is in the prodromal phase of psychosis. Research is presently underway at many institutions to try to identify those at risk so that early intervention can either prevent a full-blown psychotic state or at least minimize it.

According to the PRIME Early Intervention Clinic at Yale, early risk factors include:

- Suspiciousness or mistrust of others

- Changes in the way things look or sound
- Odd thinking or behavior
- Poor personal hygiene
- Increased difficulty at work or school
- Problems concentrating
- Difficulties thinking clearly
- Withdrawal from friends and family
- Emotional outbursts or lack of emotions
- Confusion about one's identity and future
- Feeling depressed or anxious

Add into this a family history of serious mental illness and you have all the ingredients for potentially developing schizophrenia. These concepts, however, are still experimental and a great deal of work still needs to be done before physicians are able to intervene at this early a stage.

However, it is necessary to diagnose and begin treatment early on but that is difficult because the early symptoms of schizophrenia are difficult to pick up. They can often be misinterpreted as the "normal abnormal" behavior of adolescents. What is rebellious and idiosyncratic behavior and what is pathological is sometimes difficult to distinguish in the early stages.

General symptoms include disorganized thinking, hallucinations and delusions along with social isolation. Hearing voices is common as is the individual misinterpreting the world around. These symptoms are referred to as positive symptoms because they are symptoms that are added to what we normally experience. They form the basis of psychosis. Negative symptoms are another feature of the illness and are called that because they are considered to be the loss or absence of normal traits or abilities. These include flat or blunted affect and emotion, poverty of speech called alogia, anhedonia (the inability to enjoy) and lack of motivation.

The negative symptoms are much more difficult to treat than the psychotic symptoms and lead to the chronicity of the disease. The voices and hallucinations can often be stopped with medication. The lack of emotion, poverty of speech and lack of motivation are more difficult to reverse and without those skills, it is difficult to cope well in this world. Another key symptom that many with schizophrenia develop is anosognosia or the inability to realize that you are ill. This is crucial in the issue of enforced treatment and will be discussed later at great length.

Disorganized thinking, speech, and behavior affect most people with this illness. People with schizophrenia sometimes have trouble communicating in coherent sentences or carrying on conversations with others, they may move more slowly, repeat rhythmic gestures or make movements such as walking in circles or pacing; and have difficulty making sense of everyday sights, sounds and feelings.

In addition, people with schizophrenia may also suffer panic anxiety, depression and mood swings.

To be diagnosed, a patient must have psychotic symptoms for at least six months and have increasing difficulty functioning normally. It is, however, important to do a complete physical examination in order to rule out any other condition that might cause these symptoms. Brain injury and drug use are some of the possible causes of psychotic behavior. There is, as yet, no definitive test that will demonstrate that an individual has schizophrenia. That does not, however, mean that the basis of this disease is not physical. There are many conditions that are diagnosed based on exclusion. That is, there is no other explanation therefore it must be…. Alzheimer's Disease is the prime example of a disease that is only diagnosed after all other causes for the symptoms have been ruled out.

But, even though there is no definitive test that can be used to make a diagnosis, scientists have uncovered a wealth of differences between the brains of people with schizophrenia and those who do not have the disease to demonstrate that there are numerous physical differences in the brains of those with and without the disease.

Physiological Deficits in Schizophrenia

If all the theorists who suggested that schizophrenia resulted from poor mental hygiene, bad parenting, or reactions to difficult situations were correct then those labeled schizophrenic would be no different from you or I physiologically. That, however, is not the case. More and more is being discovered about brain abnormalities in people who suffer from this disease thanks to advances in genetics and in medical imaging.

Many regions of the brain are known to operate differently in those with schizophrenia. Those differences were nicely summarized on the schizophrenia dot com website [39] The differences are:

Basal Ganglia – is involved in movement and emotions and in integrating sensory information. Abnormal functioning in this area is thought to produce paranoid symptoms and hallucinations

Frontal Lobe – is involved in critical thinking and problem solving. Changes in those with schizophrenia lead to problems planning and organizing thoughts

Limbic System – is involved with emotion and changes in schizophrenics lead to agitation

Auditory System – helps us to hear and interpret speech but in schizophrenics, overactivity in the area known as Wernicke's area can result in auditory hallucinations

Occipital Lobe – processes visual information but in schizophrenics abnormalities can produce problems in interpreting complex images, recognizing motion and reading emotions on the faces of others.

Hippocampus – mediates learning and memory formation. These are impaired in those with schizophrenia.

Neurotransmitters, the chemical messengers of the brain, and their receptors are also abnormal and therefore are a cause of schizophrenic symptoms. Too many of the neurotransmitter dopamine's receptors are present and the overabundance of them in brains of schizophrenics has been demonstrated. Other neurotransmitters may also be involved and both these issues will be discussed in the next chapter.

In 2001, scientists from the Institute of Psychiatry in Los Angeles demonstrated for the first time that the thalamus is smaller in people with schizophrenia. [40] The thalamus is considered to be the brain's sensory filter or main hub. It receives information from the various senses, filters them and passes them on to the brain for processing.

In an imaging study using magnetic resonance imaging (MRI), 68 people were examined. Thirty eight were experiencing their first episode of schizophrenia and 29 were healthy controls. The study found that there is a problem in the thalamus in those with schizophrenia. The thalamus was not properly filtering and processing the information it was receiving. This resulted in those subjects experiencing confusion – one of the symptoms of schizophrenia.

Dr. Tonmoy Sharma, who headed up the study, had previously found that people with schizophrenia also have decreased brain gray matter compared to those without the disease.

A more recent study also using MRI found both structural and functional abnormalities in specific regions of the brain amongst schizophrenics who have persistent auditory hallucinations. [41] This Spanish study looked at 31 men who were right handed. Twenty-one of them had schizophrenia and heard voices. Compared to the ten healthy controls, the men with schizophrenia displayed abnormalities and gray matter deficits in several parts of the brain that are associated with the regulation of emotion and the processing of human voices.

While these imaging studies are compelling, they often do not satisfy the anti-psychiatry types who suggest that the changes in the brain are not the result of a disease called schizophrenia. Rather, they are the result of the drugs that are given to schizophrenics. E. Fuller Torrey quotes P.R. Breggin's 1991 book entitled "Toxic Psychiatry" stating that "dozens of studies have since come out indicating that neuroleptic treated patients have such severe brain damage that it can be detected as shrinkage of the brain on the newer radiology techniques such as the CT scan......"
[42]

As recently as 2002, the science journalist Robert Whitaker wrote in his book "Mad in America" that schizophrenia is "a term loosely applied to people with widely disparate emotional problems" and he too claimed that most of the symptoms attributed to schizophrenia are caused by the drugs that these patients are given.

In order to refute these arguments, Torrey looked at all the studies carried out on people with schizophrenia who had never been treated. If they have deficits then those deficits can be attributed to the disease. In his review, summarized below, he looked at a total of 65 studies of schizophrenics never treated with antipsychotic drugs and concluded that there are significant abnormalities in both brain structure and brain function

Studies on Non Treated Schizophrenics

A. Structural Abnormalities

As early as 1809, autopsies done on brains from people with schizophrenia found that the lateral ventricles were considerably larger than normal. Then, in the 20th century, a number of studies using more sophisticated techniques called pneumoencephalography found the same. This technique involves draining most of the cerebrospinal fluid and injecting air. It enables X-rays of the brain to picture it more clearly but it is painful and is associated with numerous side effects.

Today, CT scans and MRIs are used and ten such studies have been done on patients never treated with drugs. In four of those studies, the size of the ventricles was evaluated and in all studies, the ventricles were significantly larger in schizophrenic patients compared to normal controls. The brain ventricle is the central cavity of the brain and is filled with cerebrospinal fluid. Studies of other brain structures have been inconclusive. Some studies have shown statistically significant differences or trends towards significance in some of the areas of the brain while other studies have shown no difference.

B. Neurological Abnormalities

Dyskinesias are impairments in the ability of the individual to control movements and are characterized by spasmodic or repetitive motions or lack of coordination. This condition occurs spontaneously in people with schizophrenia who have never been treated and as the result of medication. When it is the result of drugs, it is known as tardive dyskinesia. Often, the movements are of the tongue or mouth or the upper limbs.

An evaluation of the records of over 600 patients with schizophrenia in an English asylum during the period 1850 to 1890 found that over a third had movement disorders. During the early part of the 20th century, numerous psychiatrists wrote about the "marked and well-observed motor disturbances" such as "peculiar twitching of the facial muscles and myoclonic jerkings of forearms and hands".

Between 1959 and 1984, 29 or more studies assessed the prevalence of this movement disorder in untreated schizophrenics. About 5% of those studied had dyskeniesias. More recent studies put the rate at about 12% with a range of 0 to a high of 38% (in two studies).

Parkinsonian or extrapyramidal motor signs that include tremors, rigidity, and slowness of movement and resemble the symptoms of Parkinson's disease have traditionally been seen in patients with schizophrenia even though they too are ascribed to the side effects of antipsychotic medications. Since 1993, seven studies have been conducted on never treated schizophrenics. A total of 91 or 23% of the 394 patients exhibited these symptoms.

Neurological soft signs are abnormal motor or sensory findings, including involuntary movements, partial loss of the ability to coordinate and perform certain purposeful movements and gestures in the absence of motor or sensory impairments (dyspraxia), difficulties in performing rapid alternating movements, difficulties in two-point discrimination, and the inability of the individual to recognize when someone is writing on their hand (graphesthesia). These occur in people even without a neurological disorder.

These signs are found in people with a number of different central nervous system disorders including dyslexia and ADHD. In eight studies of people with schizophrenia looking at soft signs, seven included normal controls. In those studies, the subjects with schizophrenia who had never been treated had significantly more soft signs than did the controls. In two studies, treated patients had more soft signs than the untreated. This suggest that antipsychotic medications also contribute to neurologic dysfunction.

People with schizophrenia have more neurological soft signs than normal people but those signs increase when they are on medication.

It is not ethical to conduct studies of people to see how much pain they can endure but there is anecdotal evidence that people with schizophrenia do have decreased perceptions of pain. In a 1798 text, the author states that "in many cases of insanity, there prevails a great degree of insensibility, so that patients have appeared to hardly feel the application of blisters or the operation of the cup".

Similar types of observations were made in the 18th century and, in the 19th century, the famous psychiatrist, Kraeplin, noted that "patients often become less sensitive to bodily discomfort pricks of a needle injuries, without thinking much about it..." By the 1930s, this absence of pain was mentioned in all the textbooks. More recently, studies of psychotic patients who had heart attacks observed that the vast majority of them did not complain of pain.

In a Veterans Administration hospital where 79% of the residents were diagnosed with schizophrenia, there was no pain in 21% of patients with a perforated ulcer, 37% of patients with acute appendicitis and 41% of patients with a fractured femur in the leg.

Prior to the introduction of modern medications for schizophrenia and before ethical rules prevented inflicting pain on experimental subjects, some studies were conducted. In a 1955 study, 13 patients with schizophrenia were studied and they reported decreased pain perception for pinpricks or pressure. Another study inflicted thermal stimulations on 17 subjects with schizophrenia and found that they had a much lower responsiveness to that pain.

Just how many people have decreased sensitivity is not known but it is known that others may have an increased sensitivity. In some cases they have what is known as parasthesias – the feeling that insects are crawling under their skin.

Why these differences in pain perception occur is not known but it is suspected that it may involve the thalamus that is known to be abnormal in people with schizophrenia. Suggestions that this phenomenon results from the medication are ruled out by the fact that these studies were conducted and observations made before such agents existed.

C. Neuropsychological Abnormalities

Recent memory is often impaired in people with schizophrenia and this observation goes back as far as 1809. Extensive neuropsychological testing was done in the 1940s and the authors concluded that people with schizophrenia are significantly different from normal controls and from those with depression on a number of measures. More recent studies on patients never treated with antipsychotic drugs found that those with schizophrenia had a much greater impairment than normal controls on measures of verbal memory and learning. This deficit is evident as early as the first episode of the disease.

Other studies found that memory impairment was highly correlated with the level of the negative symptoms exhibited by the patients. The more pronounced the negative symptoms, the greater the amount of memory impairment. Interestingly, comparisons of those never treated with those treated found no differences in memory impairment. The medications made no difference or at least they have little effect on most neuropsychological functions.

D. Electrophysiological Abnormalities

Most people are probably aware of electroencephalograms more commonly known as EEGs. This is a method that measures the electrophysiological functions of the brain and they have been around since the early 1930s. Evaluations of these tracings are known to be somewhat subjective and it is estimated that about 10% of people will show a false abnormal reading.

In five EEG studies done to compare schizophrenics with normal controls, it was found that the range of abnormal readings for those with schizophrenia went from 23-44%. The range for the control group was 7-20%. In another study of 100 patients, it was found that abnormal readings were more pronounced in those patients whose schizophrenia was more severe.

One study before the days of medication involved placing electrodes deep into the brain of subjects. Spike abnormalities were found in the septal region, the hippocampus and the amygdala. These spikes were not found in other patients being treated for chronic pain or Parkinson's. Another similar study was done with four patients and it was found that there was abnormal electrical activity in the deep frontal and subthalmic regions.

E. Cerebral Metabolic Abnormalities

Imaging of the brain and evaluating the activity is quite new but a growing area of investigation for researchers. The three methodologies used are positron emission tomography (PET), single photon emission computed tomography (SPECT) and functional magnetic resonance imaging (fMRI).

A 2007 review of all the imaging studies done noted quite a few interesting differences. The study was published in "Schizophrenia Bulletin" July 2007 and was written by scientists from the University of Pennsylvania, Wayne State University in Detroit and the University of Edinburgh.[43]

Patients with schizophrenia, it was found, have overall brain volumes that are 3% smaller than healthy controls. This reduction in size occurs mainly in the gray area. These volume reductions are more pronounced in the frontotemporal regions while the reductions in the medial temporal lobe structures and particularly the hippocampus and amygdala and possibly the thalamus are greater than 3%. In addition, a white matter fibre bundle known as the corpus callosum is also about 3% smaller in people with schizophrenia. There is additionally an increased amount of cerebrospinal fluid (CSF) in schizophrenic patients compared to the healthy controls. The amount of CSF will increase in volume if the physical size of the brain decreases. The CSF increases to take up the space left by the reduced size of the brain.

Other imaging techniques have found that white matter structure may be disorganized rather than actually reduced in volume.

Early studies of the amygdala and the hippocampus in relatives of people with schizophrenia suggest that these two areas are smaller than in healthy controls. That reduced size, however, is not enough to cause abnormal behavior. It is not pathological. It is suspected that the reduced hippocampus might be a sign of vulnerability for schizophrenia. Reduced gray matter has also been found in relatives of schizophrenics who are at high risk for the disease and reductions in the thalamus might be another measure of genetic predisposition for psychosis.

Studies in Scotland known as the Edinburgh High Risk Study suggest that brain changes may begin to occur years prior to any diagnosis of schizophrenia. That is, long before there are any overt signs of schizophrenic behavior.

Other studies using magnetic resonance spectroscopy that look at metabolites in the brain find that there is a consistent reduction in N-acetyl-aspartate (NAA) in almost all investigations. This compound is mainly synthesized in neurons and so it is a marker for neuronal loss or dysfunction. It may also reflect the integrity of glial cells.

The reduced amounts of NAA are found mainly in the hippocampus and the frontal cortex. The reductions of NAA in these regions are associated with cortical atrophy, cognitive impairment and the negative symptoms associated with the disease. This NAA reduction is also found in close relatives.

Another finding is that there is a reduction in the generation of new cell membranes and an increase in the breakdown of existing membranes. This suggests that there is a reduction in the total number of neurons, the glia and/or the synapses.

Studies with PET and SPECT suggest an increased activity of the neurotransmitter dopamine. This increase is more pronounced in those actively psychotic and seems to be related to the positive symptoms of the disease. SPECT studies have also shown increased activity at the temporal lobe.

The effects of antipsychotic medications on the brains of people with schizophrenia have also been evaluated. These suggest that the drugs produce normalization in the brain. That is, the brains of schizophrenic patients became more like those of the healthy controls after treatment with drugs.

So, what does all this mean in terms of the symptoms and behavior of people with schizophrenia? In an editorial in the March 2007 issue of the "American Journal of Psychiatry",

[44] Dr. Robert Freedman stated "psychiatry cannot give patients a simple explanation of what is wrong with them". A number of imaging studies in that issue of the journal did try to relate neuronal dysfunction in the brains of people with schizophrenia to their symptoms but, Freedman said, "none of the articles, separately or together, gives us the all-encompassing picture of schizophrenia". But, the studies do explain many of the characteristics of people with schizophrenia and confirm many of the observations first made by psychiatrists in the 19th century.

People with schizophrenia cannot often automatically discriminate important from unimportant information. One of the studies had patients look for target stimuli on a screen while being distracted by other pictures. They were to push a button when they saw the target stimulus. The researchers found that there was decreased blood flow in the frontal cortex and the basal ganglia when subjects were shown the target stimulus. This indicates that the brain is not as active in selecting stimuli in the frontal cortex for response by the basal ganglia as it would be in normal people.

In addition, the distractor stimuli caused an over activity of blood in the inferior parietal lobe indicating that the neurons were not able to discriminate the distractions from the more important target stimulus.

The brain is said to "idle" in a default mode where there is interconnected processing of activity among the major centers of the cerebral cortex. In this study, the scientists evaluated this default activity with auditory stimuli that were defined as target stimuli and distractor stimuli. Subjects had to pick out the target sound. The interconnected network that includes the frontal, cingulated, parietal and parahippocampal cortices was studied.

70

In the normal subjects, the blood flow resonates slowly and regularly. In the schizophrenic patients, this activity is increased and is more irregular. This activity is related to the positive symptoms of the disease. The researchers concluded that the brain in schizophrenia is hyperactive in some parts and hypoactive in other parts but the entire circuit is unable to stabilize itself in the default mode.

Another of the studies looked at spontaneous brain activity when people were asleep. They found that people with schizophrenia had a deficit in sleep spindles. These are the waxing and waning oscillations at about 12-15 cycles per second that occur over the central and parietal brain areas. Sleep spindles are generated by the thalamic reticular nucleus. This is a thin sheet of inhibitory neurons between the thalamus and the cortex. This appears to be hypoactive in schizophrenics even when they sleep and plays an important role in gating and attentional modulation. That is, there is an inability to focus attention which is something that is impaired in this disease.

One study looked at the ability of people with schizophrenia to distinguish speech. Due to a diminished brain activity referred to as N1, there is a failure on the part of these patients to distinguish their own speech from that of others. Another study looked at the integrity of the connections between neuronal areas of the brain and found that there is a decrease in the pathway between Broca's motor speech area in the frontal lobe and Wernicke's receptive speech area in the temporal lobe.

People with schizophrenia have difficulty evaluating emotions in other people based on the rhythm and tone of speech (called prosody). Schizophrenics had difficulty not only in differentiating happiness versus sadness but also in determining whether a common tune was played properly or with altered notes. This is caused by a decrease in the integrity in the connections to the auditory cortex suggesting that the same types of disconnections that occur in other places in the brain also occur within simple sensory systems. Schizophrenics also had difficulty in differentiating questions from statements based upon tone of voice alone. The deficits in the ability to detect prosody may interfere with their ability to interact socially.

Hopefully, this chapter has convinced you that schizophrenia is a disease of the brain even if you, like this writer, do not fully comprehend the science of the brain imaging researchers. The individuals you see pushing a shopping cart with all their worldly belongings in it while mumbling incoherently, or shouting mostly religious rhetoric on the street corner, or living in a cardboard carton are sick people. They have a disease of the brain that can be scientifically evaluated and they should be treated as such.

The big question is what causes these changes and that will be discussed in the next chapter.

CHAPTER FOUR - THEORIES OF CAUSATION/TREATMENT

Genetics

First and foremost is the genetic explanation. A number of genes have been identified as contributing to this illness. But, that is not the complete answer. It is believed that the presence of "schizophrenia genes" gives one the susceptibility for the disease but that other factors come into play to trigger those genes to cause the illness.

If this were purely a genetic disorder then it would be expected that identical twins would both develop schizophrenia if one did (called concordance). That is not the case. Rather than 100% concordance, it is only 50%. If one identical twin develops schizophrenia, the other twin only has a 50/50 chance of developing the disease.

Those other factors that tip a person who has a genetic susceptibility into developing schizophrenia are not known but many stressors are suspected. Psychosocial stresses may be partly to blame as may be biological causes such as pregnancy and delivery complications, marijuana and infections. Both will be looked at in greater detail below. [45,46]

In fact, according to Ming Tsuang of the Harvard Medical School, a working model of schizophrenia hypothesizes that it is a neurodevelopmental disease with a strong genetic component. Genes control the embryonic neurodevelopment but the environmental insults modify that development. The interaction of the two produces the neuropathology and cognitive deficits of schizophrenia. The brain continues to develop for the next 20 or so years and is influenced by experiences. This fine tuning of the brain that continues on after childhood and into early adulthood may be negatively influenced by those environmental factors. [44]

In a 2007 interview with the medical website Medscape, Dr Nancy C Andreason, one of the leading researchers in schizophrenia stated that "the big payoff is going to be integrating information from genetics and genomics with information from imaging studies and other measures." [47] Genomics is the application of genetics to understanding how genes function together and exert their effects. Since a lot of this activity involves the production of proteins, there is now a term for that called 'proteomics'.

An even newer term is that of phenomics. People working in genetics began to realize that even with all the technology available, they still needed someone who could link genomic data to the phenotype, hence phenomics. And then there is eidomics that Dr. Andreason defines as using imaging technology to develop brain biomarkers that may help to inform about the diagnosis or treatment or the identification of neural mechanisms involved.

All of this is off in the distant future unfortunately. Currently, science is just in the process of trying to use the imaging data to understand how this disease occurs at the genetic level and how that expresses itself in brain abnormalities. We are only at the beginning, she says, with the goal that someday someone will be able to have their genetic codes evaluated and then the doctor will be able to predict what drug and the amount of that drug the person will require in order to correct the problem.

In her book, Dr. Andreason has some interesting comments about schizophrenia and creativity. She points out that people like James Joyce had a daughter with schizophrenia. Bertrand Russell had an uncle and both a son and a granddaughter with the disease. Einstein also had a son with schizophrenia. It has also been observed that a number of adopted children of schizophrenic mothers pursued creative interests suggesting that there might be a genetic association between schizophrenia and tendencies to be creative or think in original ways.

Also, while people with schizophrenia rarely marry or have children, the disease persists at an equal rate throughout the world. It just might be that schizophrenia genes may confer some evolutionary benefit that leads them to persist. Having them may transmit some abilities that are useful to humans. This is not unheard of as the sickle cell anemia gene persists because it provides protection against malaria.

It has been suggested that mild or sub-clinical schizophrenia results in people in society who are visionaries, seers and people with religious convictions. In addition, a little bit of paranoia can be a good thing.

Infectious Agents

In a 2006 article in the "Psychiatric Times" by Drs Robert H Yolken and Fuller Torrey, [48] they point out that the idea that both schizophrenia and bipolar disorder may be caused by infection was first put forth in "Scientific American" in 1896. During the 1930s, experiments were being conducted that involved injecting cerebrospinal fluid taken from people with schizophrenia into rabbit brains. Unfortunately, that study was not successful but in an e-mail to this author on that topic, Dr. Torrey said "it proves that some people were on the right track even then" In the past ten years, various reports cited the presence of infectious agents such as influenza, rubella, and bovine disease viruses along with other agents in people with both schizophrenia and bipolar disorder.

The Stanley Medical Research Institute in Chevy Chase Maryland funds the Stanley Laboratory of Developmental Neurovirology at Johns Hopkins University School of Medicine in Baltimore. Their goal is to explore the role of viruses and other infectious agents as possible causes of schizophrenia and bipolar disorder. Four infectious agents are presently being investigated as potential causes or contributory agents.

Toxoplasma Gondii

This is a theory that upsets lovers of cats as T. gondii is a protozoan parasite that lives in cats. Humans can become infected with this parasite when they ingest the oocysts that are shed by the feces of infected cats or by eating undercooked meat from an animal that came in contact with infected cat feces. Oocysts are thick walled structures that spread the parasites to a new host. These oocysts can be picked up even if you have no cat. Not only are they found in litter boxes but they are in gardens, sandboxes and other children's play areas.

T. gondii is one of the most common human parasites with about 10-20% of adults testing positive for its presence. Infection with this parasite during early pregnancy can cause severe fetal CNS abnormalities. It is now known from animal studies that exposure in late pregnancy as well can cause behavioral changes, neurologic symptoms and stillbirths.

Over 20 studies in the past number of years have looked at antibodies to T. gondii in adults with and without schizophrenia. These studies have shown that infection with T. gondii is three times greater in people with schizophrenia compared to healthy controls living in the same geographical region. Two studies found that there was an increased level of T. gondii antibodies in the late pregnancy serum of women who gave birth to children who went on to develop schizophrenia.

Other studies have shown greater childhood exposure to cats among persons with schizophrenia than among controls.

Infection with T. gondii is a viable theory for a number of reasons. [49] Genetic susceptibility is involved in the development of schizophrenia and genes are known to influence the susceptibility of animals to the influence of T. gondii. T. gondii has been shown to be transmitted across the placenta for as many as five generations in studies in mice. Schizophrenia involves abnormalities in neurotransmitters and animal studies have demonstrated an effect on dopamine and serotonin by T. gondii. Schizophrenia is also believed to be a disease of neurodevelopment and this is consistent with the parasite's ability to cause prenatal infections and remain latent for many years before becoming reactivated. That is, the infection is there but not active until years later when something triggers it. Finally, toxoplasma infections and schizophrenia is consistent with animal models that indicate persistent behavioral changes in toxoplasma infected animals.

An interesting observation is that some of the drugs used to treat psychotic symptoms have been shown to inhibit the growth of T. gondii in cell culture. In addition, there is an increase in schizophrenia amongst people born in the winter and spring months. Toxoplasmosis and many infectious diseases are also more common in the winter and spring.

Other Viruses

Herpes simplex viruses 1 and 2 are both common causes of infection in people that are spread by direct contact with someone who is infected. The most common form of HSV-1 is the cold sore. Both viruses can be spread by sexual contact but HSV-2 is mainly spread by sexual contact. Both forms of the virus can cause an inflammation of the brain called encephalitis and both are highly neurotropic. That is, they attack the nervous system.

An interesting feature of viruses from this family is that they can have a long latency period. That is, they "hide" in the body and do not display their symptoms but then flare up years after the initial infection. In this regard, they are similar to their sibling HSV-3, varicella zoster virus or chickenpox. After the active phase, the virus becomes dormant and hides in the body as well and may emerge years later as the painful disease called shingles.

One study that evaluated the mothers of patients with either schizophrenia or bipolar disease found that many of the mothers had increased levels of HSV-2 serum antibodies just before giving birth. Other studies comparing people with and without either schizophrenia or bipolar disease have found that HSV-1 infections in the ill individuals result in significant cognitive loss. This is mainly in the area of recent memory deficits. These losses were not seen in people with other forms of the herpes virus.

Cytomegalovirus (CMV) is another member of the herpes family. It is quite common also and can cause encephalitis particularly in people whose immune systems are suppressed. Studies have shown that people with schizophrenia have more antibodies to CMV than healthy controls. These antibodies have been found in both the blood and the CSF of patients. The presence of these antibodies seems to be related to the level of negative symptoms. That is, the more antibodies to CMV, the greater the degree of negative or deficit symptoms.

One trial conducted with the antiviral agent, valacyclovir, found that schizophrenic patients treated with that drug had an improvement in their symptoms.

Then there is the role of endogenous retroviruses. These are DNA elements that have become part of the human genome as the result of infection and then integration into the germ line cells of humans. These are mostly dormant but, when they become activated, they can influence the transcription of the genes above and below where they are located or integrated on the chromosome.

Genetic polymorphisms in endogenous retroviruses have been linked to alterations in immune response and an increased susceptibility to autoimmune disorders. Genetic polymorphisms are variations in a gene that codes for a single trait. This gives rise to variations in that trait, such as those seen in the human blood types. Human blood characteristics are determined by a gene but due to genetic polymorphisms of that gene, there are differences in human blood types producing types like A, O, AB and positive and negative.

These endogenous retroviruses share properties from both the normal genes and the infectious agent and are a link between the two. These retroviruses may be activated by infection with herpes virus or T. gondii. As a consequence, they may be a link between genetic causes of schizophrenia and infections.

Tick borne encephalitis (TBE) is a viral infectious disease spread like Lyme Disease by being bitten by ticks. Psychiatric symptoms that resemble schizophrenia have been observed in many of these patients. In a study conducted at the Karolinska Institute in Stockholm and reported at the Neuroscience 2007 conference in San Diego, it was found that TBE patients had a higher concentration of kynurenic acid (KYNA) in the CSF.

KYNA is believed to be associated with psychiatric symptoms in a similar manner to both angel dust (PCP) and ketamine or the date rape drug. More will be said of that below. In this particular study, it was found that the TBE patients had higher levels of KYNA than healthy controls. Other studies have found that KYNA is also elevated in the CSF and the prefrontal cortex of patients with schizophrenia. [50]

Of course, the classic case of infection-induced mental illness is syphilis. One of the main causes of mental illness before the development of antibiotics was advanced syphilis that went into the brain. Antibiotics were a magic bullet that cured early forms of this disease and prevented the progression that resulted in madness.

Marijuana

The use of cannabis has been found to be associated with an increased risk of developing schizophrenia. The classic study was that of a long term follow up of Swedish conscripts aged 18-20 in 1969-70. A total of 50,087 young people representing over 97% of that country's 18-20 male population reported on their use of cannabis, other drugs and on several other social and psychological characteristics. The researchers then looked at hospital admissions for schizophrenia amongst this group.

It was found that cannabis was associated with an increased risk of developing schizophrenia. The greater the use then the greater the risk. The researchers concluded that there was no question but that the link between the two was causal. Cannabis use caused schizophrenia and the link was not explained by the use of other psychoactive drugs or personality traits. [51]

However, it has also been hypothesized that schizophrenia leads to a greater use of marijuana likely because people are trying to medicate themselves.

A number of years after the above study was published, Scottish researchers looked at all the studies that had been done on the link between cannabis and schizophrenia between 1966 and the end of 2004. [52] That study agreed with the original findings. Early use of cannabis does appear, it said, to increase the risk of psychosis and that cannabis is an independent risk factor for both psychosis and the development of psychotic symptoms.

Again, it has been argued that prodromal symptoms of schizophrenia lead to an increased use of marijuana. Then, while the disease is developing, being stoned speeds up the developing deficits of the disease.

Neurotransmitters – Cause or Chance Treatment Focus

Up to the 1950s, there was no effective treatment for schizophrenia. The vast majority of patients lived in hospitals called asylums. If they did get treatment, it was electric or insulin shock, or lobotomies where the front part of the brain was severed from the rest of the brain. These treatments were somewhat effective only for catatonia and mania. Today, electric shock and an updated version called transcranial magnetic stimulation are being researched and used for depression. They are applied more humanely as well.

In 1950, a French pharmaceutical company developed a drug called chlorpromazine for use as an antihistamine for allergies and as an anti nausea treatment. The nausea sensation begins in the vomiting center of the brain. It was quickly noted that this drug caused extreme sedation similar to that produced by narcotic drugs. Patients were also relieved of most of their anxiety. [53]

In 1952, two French physicians published a study of the effects of this drug on 38 psychotic patients. The patients improved in both their thinking and their emotional behavior. Chlorpromazine and similar compounds that followed was the first reasonably effective treatment for schizophrenia. Haldol or haloperidol is probably the most well known and this class of drugs is commonly referred to as typical antipsychotics. More will be said about that later. The development of reasonably effective drug therapy helped give impetus to a growing movement to discharge people from asylums although the process of deinstitutionalization as it is called did go overboard. Much more will be said about that process in a later chapter.

Very often, medicine is able to control the symptoms of disease with drugs but they really have no idea why or how those drugs work. The drugs do seem to work by controlling the symptoms and so they are prescribed. That was the case with the typical antipsychotics. Unfortunately, they also caused considerable side effects called parkinsonism symptoms. People who took them at too high doses or for too long developed the symptoms of Parkinson's disease such as rigidity and tremors.

The most severe symptom, tardive diskinesia (TD) is characterized by repetitive, involuntary, and purposeless movements such as grimacing, tongue protrusion, lip smacking, puckering and pursing, and rapid eye blinking. Rapid movements of the arms, legs, and trunk may also occur. These cannot be reversed. As mentioned earlier, some of these symptoms are also associated with schizophrenia even when these drugs are not being used.

In 1963, Dr. Philip Seeman was a Canadian doctor, trained at McGill in Montreal, and doing research for a PhD at Rockefeller University in New York City. His wife, Mary was a psychiatrist quoted in chapter one of this book. She took Philip with her to the Manhattan State Hospital. Dr. Philip stated in an essay he wrote in 2001 [54] that the sight of 2000 patients with schizophrenia or psychosis was unforgettable. His wife said "why don't you do something useful? Why don't you find the cause of schizophrenia?"

That challenge set him on a lengthy journey to discover how the antipsychotic drugs worked. Now a professor at the University of Toronto and one of the world's top schizophrenia researchers, Dr. Seeman did find his answer in 1974 and 1975. But first we need some definitions. Neurotransmitters are chemical messengers in the brain. Neurons in the brain do not physically touch but they are separated by gaps called synapses. To talk to each other, one neuron releases the appropriate messenger (of which there are many) to take the message to the next neuron. That neurotransmitter attaches itself to a receptor that is designed only for that particular receptor and the neurotransmitter is then disposed of.

One important neurotransmitter is dopamine, and Parkinson's disease is caused when the amount of dopamine in the brain becomes severely depleted. That depletion is what causes the familiar symptoms of that disease.

What Philip Seeman discovered was that antipsychotic drugs blocked a dopamine receptor that he called the D2 receptor. It was then discovered that people with schizophrenia have more of these receptors than normal. Psychotic symptoms are relieved when the drug blocks the receptor and prevents dopamine from binding. The longer an antipsychotic drug blocks these receptors, the more potent it is in reducing psychotic symptoms.

More recently, it has been discovered that in people with schizophrenia, there is a supersensitivity to dopamine. [55] It was also discovered that the older antipychotic medications (the typical antipsychotics) blocked the dopamine receptors more extensively and for longer periods of time than the newer drugs called atypical antipsychotics.

The therapeutic action of the drugs occurs when 65% to 85% of brain D2 receptors are occupied. When more than 78% or 80% of the D2 receptors are occupied then the side effects associated with the typical drugs occur. The atypical drugs occupy less of the receptors. The length of time that the drug occupies the receptor is also important. The older drugs stay on the receptor much longer than the newer ones thus these newer drugs have fewer parkinsonism side effects.

Haldol stays on the D2 receptor for 38 minutes, chlorpromazine for 30 minutes but clozapine for only 15 seconds and quetiapine for 16 seconds. This short time period is still long enough to interrupt dopamine but to then allow enough to get through to avoid the side effects. It is believed that only a few hours a day of 60-70% D2 occupancy is sufficient to relieve psychotic symptoms.

Of course, these newer drugs do have other side effects as mentioned earlier. They can cause extreme weight gain, type 2 diabetes, elevated cholesterol levels and sexual side effects such as impotence and disrupted menstruation.

The existing antipsychotics that only influenced the dopamine system tend to be only effective for the treatment of the positive symptoms of schizophrenia and are not effective for the negative ones. This has led to the consideration that other neurotransmitters might also be involved with the disease. Some of the newer atypical antipsychotics that have been developed recently influence not only the dopaminergic systems but also effect serotonin - another of the neurotransmitters in the brain. These newer drugs reduce dopamine activity in some parts of the brain and increase serotonin activity in other parts.

The Angel Dust/PCP Theory

Over the past few years, attention has been focused on the glutamatergic system involving agents that block N-methyl-d-aspartate or NMDA. [56] Glutamic acid is the major excitatory neurotransmitter in the brain involving 40% of all synapses. Two street drugs, PCP (angel dust) and ketamine (the date rape drug) are known to cause behavior that closely resembles that of schizophrenia. These drugs block the NMDA receptors. In fact, the psychosis induced by both PCP and ketamine very closely resembles schizophrenia because they not only produce positive symptoms but also the negative symptoms and cognitive deficits that are so resistant to treatment in schizophrenia.

Post mortem evaluations of the brains of people with schizophrenia have shown that they have fewer NMDA receptors than people who do not have the disease. Both glycine and d-serine (that increase the levels of NMDA) have been found to be decreased in both the blood and cerebrospinal fluid of people with schizophrenia compared to controls. This has all led to the hypothesis that people with schizophrenia have too little NMDA and that is one cause of some of the symptoms of the disease – particularly the negative symptoms and the cognitive deficits.

This knowledge has lead to a number of investigations evaluating the effect of various agents that will increase the amount of NMDA in the brains of those with schizophrenia

Glycine is known to act as an agonist for NMDA. That is it mimics NMDA. Glycine is an amino acid that is found in the protein of all living things. The normal human diet results in an intake of about two grams of glycine daily. It is believed that supplementing with glycine may not only have antispastic activity but it may also have antipsychotic activity along with anti-oxidant and anti-inflammatory properties.

A number of small, randomized control trials have been done looking at the effect of adding glycine to atypical antipsychotics and the impact that would have on symptoms. In January 2005, a team of Finnish researchers published a meta-analysis in "Schizophrenia Research" (Vol 72, Issues 2-3, pages 225-234). A meta-analysis combines the results from all studies and re-analyzes the data. This has the advantage of increasing the sample size by combining studies.

In this case, there were 18 short-term trials included in the meta-analysis involving 343 patients who were given various NMDA agonist compounds in addition to their antipsychotics. The study found that both glycine and D-serine (another amino acid synthesized in the body from glycine) were effective in reducing negative symptoms but that the magnitude of the effect was small.

Two other recent trials were published in "Biological Psychiatry" in 2004 and 2005. The first was by Uriel Heresco-Levy and colleagues. Seventeen patients on either olanzapine or risperidone were given 8 g/day of glycine in addition to their regular medications for a 6-week period. Patients were then switched. If they were getting placebo during the first six weeks, they received glycine in the second phase and vice versa. The trial was blind so that neither the researchers nor the patients knew what was being taken.

It was found that glycine was well tolerated by the patients and that there was a significant reduction in negative symptoms. The size of the sample, however, was small and the length of the study was short but the researchers did conclude that the efficacy of risperidone and olanzapine might be augmented using high dose adjuvant glycine treatment.

The second study was also conducted by Dr. Heresco-Levy and involved the use of D-serine as an add-on with the same two drugs as the previous research. The sample size was larger at 39 and patients were given 30 mg/Kg/day of D-serine added to their regular medications.

The researchers found that there were significant improvements in negative, positive, cognitive and depression symptoms. While gylcine and D-serine both act as NMDA agonists, there are differences between them. Glycine passes the blood brain barrier with greater difficulty and thus more of it must be taken in order for it to reach the brain than D-serine. However, D-serine has been found to cause kidney damage in rats and, until its safety has been determined, it is not approved for clinical use in the U.S.

Some rather disappointing results were obtained with the as yet unpublished multi-center study called "Cognitive and Negative Symptoms in Schizophrenia Trial" (CONSIST). This study (the largest to date) was designed to evaluate the efficacy of either glycine or d-cycloserine (a partial NMDA agonist) as an add-on to antipsychotics other than clozapine. The study involved 135 subjects for a 16-week period.

While no significant effects were found for either study compound, Dr. Daniel Javitt told a workshop at the American Psychiatric Association (APA) meeting in Toronto in May 2006 that the findings were "not all doom and gloom". There were some interesting subgroup findings. A subgroup analysis found that there was a significant reduction in symptoms amongst in-patients treated with glycine. This is consistent with earlier studies that all used in-patients rather than outpatients. Why this was the case is not known.

Another possible problem was that the dosing was lower in this study. Glycine should be given at the rate of 0.8 g per kilogram of body weight but in this study all patients received 60 g per day of glycine. Also, in the earlier studies, the serum levels of glycine reached 1000 nmol/ml but in this study it only reached 600 nmol/ml. Clearly, more studies on glycine dosing need to be done.

A more positive pilot study on patients in the prodromal phase of schizophrenia who were given glycine was sufficiently positive that it was halted early and a randomized placebo controlled trial begun.

According to Scott W. Woods of the PRIME early intervention clinic at Yale University speaking at the same conference, schizophrenia develops from premorbid to prodromal to fully psychotic. There is, he said, likely a progression of pathophysiologic mechanisms involved in the disease. Treatment targeting mechanisms operating during the prodromal phase could prevent progression of the illness and the development of full psychosis.

The study he described that was conducted at Yale looked at the role that glycine might have in preventing progression of the disease in patients who exhibited prodromal symptoms. Glycine occurs naturally in the body and is available as a supplement. Consequently, 10 subjects were selected and treated with 0.8 g/kg of glycine for eight weeks. The glycine proved to be very effective at reducing symptoms and demonstrated better results than were found with a similar study using olanzapine. Many of the patients met the criteria for full remission after eight weeks of treatment.

As a result of these positive findings, the pilot study was halted and a 12 week randomized trial is now recruiting subjects. The caveat for the pilot study is that it was an open label trial without placebo and more realistic findings will be obtained from the placebo study.

The studies described above are all using NMDA agonists but there is another possible method that might be successful at increasing levels of NMDA. That is the use of an NMDA antagonist that would work like the current SSRI anti-depressants. The current class of anti-depressants work by preventing serotonin from being degraded after it has done its job. When serotonin, or any other neurotransmitter, delivers its message across the synapse and reaches the receptor on the next neuron, it is eliminated or neutralized. The SSRIs prevent that from happening thus enabling more serotonin to remain in the brain. They are serotonin antagonists.

Similarly, it may be possible to increase the synaptic availability of glycine by inhibiting its re-uptake through a compound called the glycine transporter – 1 or GlyT-1. Sacrasine is a natural amino acid that appears to have those properties. In one study this hypothesis was successfully tested.

Dr. Guochuan Tsai and his colleagues completed their double blind randomized control trial on 36 patients with schizophrenia who were being treated with antipsychotics. Patients were assigned to receive either 2 g/day of sarcosine or placebo. Sarcosine outperformed placebo. There was a 17% reduction in positive symptoms with sarcosine compared to placebo, a 14% reduction in the negative symptoms and a 13% improvement in cognition compared to placebo. There were no differences in side effects.

Another small trial comparing sarcosine to D-serine as add-on treatments was also positive. In this study, also done by Dr. Tsai and his colleagues, 65 subjects were randomized to risperidone plus placebo, risperidone plus D-serine or risperidone plus sarcosine. The sarcosine group had greater reduction on the PANSS total score than either placebo or D-serine. On the SANS test, sarcosine was also superior to the two other study arms. PANSS stands for positive and negative symptoms in schizophrenia and is a test given to evaluate changes in symptoms.

Dr. Tsai who presented his data at another workshop at the APA and who was interviewed at the time by this author stated that "this study indicates that sarcosine....may be more efficacious than NMDA glycine site agonists for adjuvant treatment of schizophrenia at least in the acute phase".

Ampakines are subtypes of receptors that recognize glutamate and are involved in a process known as long-term potentiation, or LTP that is involved with memory. It is believed that AMPA receptor activity modulated with Ampakine drugs may provide a new and highly affective approach to treating a number of central nervous system disorders such as Alzheimer's disease and schizophrenia.

This is the research direction that Dr. Donald C Goff of Harvard is taking. He told the APA workshop in 2006 that ampakines are able to open the gated NMDA channels in the brain by depolarization. That is, changing the membrane cells electrically to become more positive. This has the effect of removing the magnesium blockade, opening the channel and allowing more NMDA to be present.

There are a number of different ampakines but he conducted his research on a compound called CX516 that he admitted was a low potency ampakine with a very short half-life.

In this study,105 patients were randomized to continue to receive their usual antipsychotic with the add on of either a placebo or 300 mg of CX516 three times/day for four weeks. While the analysis showed no difference in the composite cognitive score, there were interesting differences between those taking clozapine and those on other atypical antipsychotics. Those on clozapine and the ampakine had a worsening of their symptoms that approached statistical significance. The patients on the ampakine and other atypicals did show an improvement in cognitive symptoms that approached significance.

Dr. Goff suggested that the poor results might have been the result of using an ampakine that is not very potent and that more potent compounds may prove to be beneficial. He also pointed out that the negative results with patients taking clozapine might be caused by the fact that clozapine may also be an NMDA agonist. This possibility has been mentioned by other researchers as clozapine is the only antipsychotic that improves negative symptoms and cognition.

From the preliminary studies that are being conducted, this avenue does show considerable promise. However, if anyone does wish to try glycine, it is highly recommended that it only be done in consultation with the doctor and that the glycine used is made to either prescription or pharmaceutical grade standards. Clinical trials have begun with 15 gm per day and the dose is then increased by 15 gm per day every three days until a total dose of 60 gm/day has been achieved. This dose is based upon an average weight for the individual of about 150 pounds.

It is not recommended to try this if you are on clozapine.

A research team from the University of California San Diego found a link between an inflammatory enzyme complex called NADPH oxidase and the dysfunction of certain brain neurons exposed to ketamine. NADPH oxidase is normally found in white blood cells circulating outside the brain where it helps kill bacteria and fungus by producing superoxide. This superoxide can cause substantial damage to cells.

It turns out that superoxide is also responsible for modulating signaling in the brain. When ketamine blocks the NMDA receptors, it also increases the activity of NADPH oxidase causing further disruption of neuronal signaling. The increased excitation of NADPH leads to the production of more superoxide resulting in detrimental changes in key synaptic proteins and then profoundly affecting nervous system functions.

This then results in impairment of the brain circuitry involved with memory, attention, and other functions associated with learning. When the researchers blocked the activity of NADPH oxidase with an inhibitor or with a compound that neutralizes superoxide in mice brains, the neurons were protected.

The researchers suggest that these findings might lead to future therapies for schizophrenia. Their results were published in the Dec 7, 2007 issue of the journal "Science" [57].

Other Neurotransmitters

There is now some evidence to suggest that the cholinergic system is also involved in schizophrenia. This is the system in the brain that communicates with the neurotransmitter acetylcholine. This neurotransmitter is involved with memory function and is reduced in people with Alzheimer's Disease. This chemical binds to both muscarinic acid and nicotinic receptor and may help to explain why about 80% of people with schizophrenia smoke. [58]

Smoking might possibly provide a metabolic boost that decreases the intensity of side effects associated with their medications. It might also be because smoking activates deficient nicotinic receptors. In certain parts of the brain of schizophrenics, there is a decreased alpha 7 nicotinic receptor binding. Other studies suggest that sensory gating which is a function related to attention and the ability to filter out extraneous information is deficient in schizophrenics. The alpha 7 receptor also mediates this.

Regardless of the physiologic reason for smoking, ask any person with schizophrenia why they smoke and they will usually answer that it makes them feel better and think more clearly.

And Now some Controversy

Coming up with right idea at the right time is crucial and this is a case where what might be a good idea was suggested and researched at the wrong time. Even mentioning this theory will get the author into hot water but science does have an ethical obligation to properly evaluate a potential treatment if that treatment seems to be effective or rational.

If you have high cholesterol, your doctor might suggest that you take niacin or its other form niacinamide. Niacin can cause uncomfortable flushes in the body (like hot flashes) but the niacinamide version does not. These are both members of the vitamin B family – B3 to be specific. Treatment with vitamin B3 by a cardiologist or other physician treating high cholesterol today is considered mainstream medicine.

Should you ever happen to mention trying vitamin B3 for schizophrenia to a mental health specialist, you will be very quickly dismissed and told that there is no evidence for this treatment whatsoever. What is called orthomolecular psychiatry is bunk, they will tell you. And yet, the physician who discovered the use of niacin for cholesterol is better known (or infamous) for his research into the use of niacin for schizophrenia.

The efficacy of B3 as a valuable treatment is accepted in one branch of medicine but vilified in the other. And yet, as the section above suggested, research is taking place on an amino acid for schizophrenia. Amino acids are often lumped into the same category as vitamins.

The doctor in question is Abram Hoffer who worked with Dr Humphrey Osmond. Hoffer began practicing psychiatry in Saskatchewan in the early 1950s but before becoming an MD and then a psychiatrist, he obtained a PhD in microbiology from the University of Minnesota. He worked researching vitamin content in cereals.

Osmond is the person who coined the term psychedelic during his research with LSD and is the one who supplied the writer, Aldous Huxley, with that agent. Both he and Hoffer were interested in the role of LSD and mescaline because of the similarity in effects that both drugs produce to the symptoms of schizophrenia.

Osmond joined Hoffer in Saskatchewan and eventually moved to the US as director of the Bureau of Research in Neurology and Psychiatry at the New Jersey Psychiatric Institute in Princeton and then he became a professor of psychology at the University of Alabama. Hoffer went into private practice in Regina and then moved to Victoria, British Columbia. Osmond passed away in 2004 at the age of 86 but at the time of writing this book, Hoffer is still practicing in Victoria. He has just published his memoirs where the theory they developed together is explained [37]

While B3 is central to his hypothesis, this is not a simple matter of "vitamins curing all" that is so often promoted by the so-called alternative health people. Vitamins are chemicals in the body that have a function and Hoffer looked at the role one of them played as you will see below.

Mescaline and other hallucinogens produce symptoms that are similar to schizophrenia. Consequently, the Hoffer group looked for an agent in the body that they called factor M - something similar to mescaline that produced schizophrenia. They knew that the structure of adrenaline is similar to hallucinogens as they are all compounds based on the two-ring indole structure.

They also knew that when asthmatics inhaled adrenaline for their symptoms they sometimes developed side effects similar to that of ingesting LSD. This occurred when the adrenaline had gone from a clear color to pink. This pink adrenaline is an oxidized derivative of adrenaline called adrenochrome and it is very unstable. If the lost electron from oxidation is replaced, adrenochrome will convert back to adrenaline.

However, if the lost electron is not replaced or there is a deficiency in the nicotinamide adenine dinucleotide (NAD) system then the oxidized adrenaline will lose another electron. When this happens, the compound cannot be converted back to adrenaline. It becomes very reactive and converts to adrenolutin and other oxidized indoles. It was further hypothesized that supplements of B3 (nicotinamide) might limit the formation of adrenochrome by competitively inhibiting the action of NAD.

Adrenochrome slows what is called the Krebs cycle. These are a series of enzymatic reactions that strip energy from glucose in small increments so that the sugars are not burned in one big flame. It was thought that the inhibition of the Krebs cycle by adrenochrome could lead to the symptoms of mental illness.

Thus, the hypothesis that they developed was:

1. Noradrenaline combines with a methyl group to produce adrenaline

2. Adrenaline loses two electrons to become adrenochrome

3. Adrenochrome produces schizophrenia

They knew that B3 is a methyl acceptor and so it might decrease the formation of adrenaline from noradrenaline as produced in step one above. A decrease in adrenaline would result in a decrease in adrenochrome. Also, B3 is a major component of NAD thus large doses of B3 would regenerate NAD and counter the poisoning effect of adrenochrome.

In one small double blind study, patients were given either a placebo, niacinamide or niacin. Because niacin can cause a flush and those patients taking that could be identified if they flushed, the nurses involved in the study were told that the patients were either on niacin or a placebo but not on niacinamide. They would assume that those on niacinamide were on placebo.

The result was that 3 of the 9 on placebo were well. Eight of the ten on niacin and 9 of 11 on niacinamide were well. This data, however, met with considerable skepticism. Other researchers tried to replicate the data but were unable to do so. Hoffer claims that they did not study newly diagnosed patients and/or did not follow his research protocols because of an inherent bias.

After years of controversy, the American Psychiatric Association wrote a report in 1973 refuting the Hoffer orthomolecular approach.

There is much of interest in Hoffer's memoirs and his biochemical theory sounds plausible but there were also aspects of his memoirs that bothered this author. Additionally, and more will be said about the alternative medicine people in a later chapter, the vitamin people seem to have taken what he said and gone to extremes.

A posting on a health food blog/website [59] refers to Hoffer and orthomolecular psychiatry and suggests this regimen be followed for good mental health:

After the morning meal take:

- A multivitamin tablet

- 1,000 mg of vitamin B-3 (as niacinamide or inositol hexanicotinate)
- One B-complex tablet with100 mg of vitamin B-6 1,200 mcg of vitamin B-9 (folate or folic acid)
- 1,000-2,000 IU of vitamin D (the lower number if you get sunshine, the higher number if you don't)
- 1,000 mg of vitamin C
- 200 mg of magnesium
- 50 mg of zinc
- 200 micrograms (mcg) of selenium
- 30 grams of soy protein powder and
- one tablespoon of lecithin granules mixed into a small glass of juice or milk
- A supplement of omega-3 fatty acids [eicosapentaenoic acid (EPA), docosahexanoic acid (DHA) and alpha-linolenic acid (ALA)]

After the midday meal:

- 1,000 mg of vitamin B-3
- 1,200 mg of vitamin folate
- 100 mg of vitamin B-6
- One B-complex tablet
- 1,000 mg of vitamin C
- 200 mg of magnesium

After the evening meal:
- A multivitamin tablet
- 1,000 mg of vitamin B-3
- 1,000 mg of vitamin C
- One B-complex tablet
- 100 mg of vitamin B-6

All of this will stave off mental disorders. More on vitamins and alternative medicine in a later chapter but all of this can only help to further discredit Hoffer and his theories in the minds of mainstream medicine and science.

However, the issue is not dead as some researchers are again looking at this approach. A study in Israel is now recruiting patients. The study authors state that "controlled studies using the orthomolecular approach have been few. Those that were done were performed in chronic schizophrenia or in populations that included bipolar and schizoaffective patients. Both of these diagnostic groups are not today considered to benefit from the orthomolecular approach. Moreover, some negative studies of high-dose niacin were done in patients who were not otherwise given general counseling for good diet as described above. Therefore, this proposal is to study in a controlled manner carefully defined first onset schizophrenic patients using the protocol advocated by Osmond and Hoffer." [60]

The study is presently recruiting subjects and all of them will be taking the antipsychotic medication risperidone and will receive dietary counseling. The study patients will be given niacinamide (B3), pyridoxine (B6) and ascorbate (vitamin C) while the control group will be given the multivitamin Centrum Forte.

However, a caution. If anyone does want to try B vitamins, make sure that you tell your psychiatrist and do not go off prescribed medication.

CHAPTER FIVE – BEYOND CHLORPROMAZINE

Deinstitutionalization

Health care officials must have been ecstatic in the 1950s when it was discovered that chlorpromazine was an effective drug against what they probably considered the worst symptoms of schizophrenia – the positive ones of delusions, hallucinations and voices. They undoubtedly saw these drugs as an opportunity to empty their asylums which were coming under increasing criticism.

Originally, the asylum system was seen as a humane way to treat people with mental illnesses. Fuller Torrey makes reference to an 1824 New York State Legislature report that describes how people with mental illnesses are passed from town to town to get rid of them. Often, they are just dumped in town squares. [8]

During the 1800s, psychiatric hospitals emphasized humane or moral treatments. Hospitals only had a few hundred patients and inhabitants were given adequate food and exercise. Rather than using physical restraints, the moral treatment utilized kindness, firmness and structure with an underpinning of conservative Christian principals. But then, the number of patients began to explode and, as an example, between 1880 and 1950 the population of these hospitals increased 13 fold compared to only a three fold increase in the total population of the US.

In his book, "The Invisible Plague", [61] Torrey examines data from the US, Canada, England and Ireland and demonstrates that from about 1750 on there was an enormous increase in the number of people with serious mental illnesses. Why this happened is not known but in an interview, Torrey suggested the following:

"The increase does appear to coincide with industrialization and especially urbanization in general and is almost certainly biological. Our own research has investigated infectious agents as a cause of schizophrenia and manic-depressive illness, and that theory fits nicely with the observed rise in insanity. Other biological factors that should be considered include changes in diet and exposure to toxins." [61]

An alternate explanation is that in agrarian times characterized by small villages and farms, those who were different in behavior – the mentally handicapped and the psychotics – were more easily accommodated and tolerated as long as they remained predictable. When not predictable they were sent away and wandered from village to village. Or, they were punished and they died young. Those who wandered were often provided sanctuary by religious organizations like Quakers or nuns.

Because of this huge surge in residents, the asylums that were initially built for humane reasons "had become on the best of days merely human warehouses. On the difficult days they became much worse than that." [8, P 82] The 1948 movie, "The Snake Pit", with Olivia DeHavilland showed the world a very graphic portrait of what life was like in an asylum of that day.

But four years earlier, in 1944, a grand jury was established to investigate the condition in the Cleveland State Hospital. This was precipitated by a series of articles in 1943 in the Cleveland Press. Conditions that were described included the beating and shackling of patients, inadequate food, overcrowding, poor salaries for staff and the neglect of treatment.

It was reported that patients with TB were put into a room with no sunlight or ventilation and that four women were put into seclusion rooms and left until they all came down with pneumonia. They were only discovered on the day they died when they all had very high fevers. Patients who had died, it was stated, were left in a makeshift morgue where rats ate off their faces while they waited burial [8]

What had been set up as places of humane care had become Snake Pits as described in the film.

The "whistle blowers" who provided the newspaper with this information were conscientious objectors (Quakers, Mennonites and Methodists) working in the asylum in place of war duty.

Because of the articles and the grand jury findings, the superintendent of the hospital was fired, more money was given to them and reforms were undertaken. This victory led to the investigation of other asylums. When the war ended in 1945, the conscientious objectors established a National Reform Movement that included such luminaries as Pearl S Buck, Eleanor Roosevelt, Robert Oppenheimer, Henry R. Luce and others.

Thanks to Luce, Life Magazine carried stories on the condition of asylums with titles like "Bedlam 1946: Most US Mental Hospitals are a Shame and a Disgrace". The story was accompanied by pictures of hospital day rooms filled with naked patients. These exposés led to the creation of the National Institute of Mental Health.

All of this, coupled with the finding of chlorpromazine, led to what has become known as the deinstitutionalization movement and the moving of the mentally ill out of asylums and into the community. It was intended as a humane act but, for the most part, it has been a failure.

As the Scientist Magazine said in its December 2007 special supplement on schizophrenia, "most of the money that had been spent caring for mentally ill people in hospitals never made it out into the community mental health system." They were quoting Kenneth Dudek, president of Fountain House in New York City. [58] Additionally, the cost of large asylums is considerably less than the money needed to provide adequate service in the community.

A 2001 "Journal of Rehabilitation" article on deinstitutionalization concluded that "various historical factors contributed to deinstitutionalization of persons with SMI. While the underlying philosophy behind deinstitutionalization was noble, it has not been entirely beneficial to persons with SMI. Treatment is often fragmented and negative societal attitudes have been detrimental to the success of deinstitutionalization. It is difficult to implement social change without adequate support at the community level". [63]

Not unexpectedly, Fuller Torrey is a bit more blunt. He states on his website that "deinstitutionalization...... has been a major contributing factor to increased homelessness, incarceration and acts of violence".

In his book, Torrey returns to Ohio for another example of a grand jury that met 50 years after the initial grand jury investigated conditions in the mental hospitals. This time, they were investigating the 1994 conditions of mentally ill people in Ohio's prison system. The Cleveland Plain Dealer described the report as reading "like a Charles Dickens novel: tales of naked men and women languishing in fetid cells, sometimes without heat or hot water or being punished for behavior that appears to be the result of their mental illness".[8P 84]

The pioneers of the deinstitutionalization movement later expressed regret at what they had done. Seymour Kaplan said that "it was the gravest error he had ever made"[8, P 86]. Donald Langsley was quoted as saying that "those of us who were once so enthusiastic now weep a little as we look backwards at what has happened to the promising child of the 1960s and early 1970s."[8 P 86]

One problem according to Torrey is that this experiment was launched based on a single study involving only 20 selected patients. This was an English study done in 1960 in which high functioning schizophrenic patients who were able to work were discharged from hospital to a community setting. They did not represent the typical schizophrenic patients but this study is referred to by all advocates of deinstitutionalization as what it is possible to accomplish. An unrepresentative sample of 20 led to a policy that resulted in 92% of all patients in American (and equal percentages in other countries) being discharged into the community.

Five other studies completed before 1981 were evaluated and three of them were methodologically flawed. As Torrey says so vehemently "it is doubtful that ever in the history of modern medicine has such a profound change in the treatment for so many sick people been implemented with so little scientific justification".[8 P 86]

The same movement as in the US also took place in other countries of the world. Patients were shifted from psychiatric hospitals into the community without the requisite supply of supports to keep those patients healthy. The World Health Organization pointed out in a 2001 report that this direction of closing hospitals in many countries was not and is not being accompanied by the development of community services. This has led to what they called a "service vacuum" [64]

The early deinstitutionalization reformers were probably buoyed by the discovery of antipsychotic medications. They likely saw these drugs as a "magic bullet" that would allow people with schizophrenia to be freed from their delusions and their voices and to be able to reintegrate back into society. While these drugs did remove the delusions and hallucinations for most people or, at least, reduce them to levels that were bearable, they had no effect on the negative symptoms.

With cognitive problems like memory loss, inability to differentiate the subtle meanings involved in human communication, lack of motivation, depression and the other symptoms of the disease, it is hard to function successfully in the real world. Considerable training and supports are needed to help people function.

Dr. Jeffrey Leiberman, chair of psychiatry at Columbia University and director of the New York State Psychiatric Institute said that "people have to get reacclimated and reoriented and they need help in doing so". [58] This sort of help and support is as important as medication. People also need housing, vocational and psychosocial rehabilitation.

But there are barriers other than a lack of funding

Anosognosia

Understanding that you are ill and that you need treatment is essential in order to improve. This is known as having insight into your illness. Without that, patients will not take their medication and do those other things that will help them. The term that describes this is anosognosia – a condition whereby someone denies or seems unaware that they are sick.

This condition is fairly common following brain injury and strokes but it can exist in conjunction with just about any neurological ailment. People will come up with all manner of strange explanations to account for their illness or injury. Xavier Amador, a psychologist at the New York State Psychiatric Institute, in an article from the Psychiatric News refers to a study that found that 89% of patients with schizophrenia denied having an illness.[65] In his own study, he found that about 60% of people with schizophrenia did not consider themselves ill.

The insights that are most vulnerable to severe mental illness are:

- the awareness that a person is even suffering from a mental illness
- the effects of medications
- the social consequences of having a mental disorder

As an example of the concept anosognosia, Amadore provides the following example from someone not with schizophrenia but with a lesion.

This individual had a lesion on the frontal lobe of his brain but was unaware that he was paralyzed on his left side or that he had problems writing. When asked to draw a clock, the patient thought that he had done a good job. When he was told that the numbers were on the outside, the patient denied that it was even his drawing.

This lack of awareness of illness on the part of those with schizophrenia leads to lack of compliance with medications. If they do not believe that they are ill then why would they take drugs or do anything else associated with treatment?

Should we, as a society, force them to accept treatment?

The lawyers and the civil libertarians say no. Unless very strict conditions are met, people have a right to remain insane. Others argue that people have a right to become well and if they do not know they are sick then they should be treated regardless. It may also be the preponderance of lawyers being in charge. That is not a profession with any kind of mandate to help care for people or to provide for them.

Involuntary Treatment

Protecting the rights of the individual is crucial and necessary in our society. Our laws and our institutions ensure that no one is imprisoned needlessly and that all have due process and protection. On the other hand, society itself needs to be protected and so a fine balance exists between protecting the individual and protecting society.

In the case of those who are mentally ill, we seem to be erring on allowing too many protections and that has a negative impact on those individuals as well. Unless very stringent rules governing involuntary hospitalization and forced treatments are met, sick people are allowed the right to not be treated even if they are so ill that they do not even know they are ill.

With the exception of many families of the seriously mentally ill, psychiatrists and the police, most feel that this is suitable. The criteria used to determine if someone can be treated by force or confined against their will varies by jurisdiction. By states in the US and by province in Canada. However, the basic rules are that the individual must be seen as a potential threat to himself or others. In some jurisdictions, these have been expanded slightly and usually in reaction to some horrific case.

Brian's Law in Ontario and Kendra's Law in New York State are two examples of the liberalizing of legislation in response to events. Brian's Law is named after the Ottawa TV sportscaster, Brian Smith, who was murdered by a seriously mentally ill man. The new legislation expands the conditions for committal to hospital by removing the word "imminent". The individual does not have to be an imminent danger to himself and/or others but simply a danger.

The police no longer have to actually observe this dangerous behavior but can determine that it exists as the result of interviewing family and friends. The law also allows for community treatment orders for discharged mental patients. This is an agreement with the patient or his/her decision maker to ensure that the patient continues treatment and medication after discharge. If not, then the person is returned to hospital.

Just getting these small changes enacted resulted in considerable debate and they probably would not have been approved if Brian Smith had not been such a public figure.

Kendra's Law is named for Kendra Webdale, a young woman who was killed after being pushed in front of a New York city subway in 1999 by a mentally ill man. This law enables the state to obtain a court order to ensure what is called assisted outpatient treatment for persons who are mentally ill and who in view of their treatment history and present circumstances, are unlikely to survive safely in the community without supervision.

Unfortunately, having someone committed and ensuring that they receive treatment in most jurisdictions in North America is difficult. But then, the consequences for the individuals and society are even more problematic.

As we saw earlier, people who are not treated tend to be homeless and/or in jail. Protecting the rights of individuals and respecting their decision to not be treated is one thing but when that results in them setting up home in a old appliance carton in an alley or sleeping on a heating grate in winter in one of our cities, it is unfair. It is unfair to allow them to be sick when they do not have the capacity to rationally make the decision not to be sick and it is unfair to their families to make them see a loved one in such despair.

What is surprising is that we allow people who are not capable of making a rational treatment decision do so even when it means that they will be forced to endure the pain of imaginary voices, delusions and hallucinations, homelessness, poverty and all else that comes with non treatment. However, we do not let people who are of sound mind but who are suffering with a terminal illness end their suffering through assisted suicide.

Another consequence of not forcing treatment is violence according to data on the Treatment Advocacy Center website [66]

In the US there are approximately 1,000 homicides among the estimated 20,000 total homicides in the U.S. committed each year by people with untreated schizophrenia and manic-depressive illness. According to a 1994 Department of Justice, Bureau of Justice Statistics Special Report, "Murder in Families," 4.3 percent of homicides committed in 1988 were by people with a history of untreated mental illness (study based on 20,860 murders nationwide).

The Department of Justice report also found:

- of spouses killed by spouse – 12.3 percent of defendants had a history of untreated mental illness;
- of children killed by parent – 15.8 percent of defendants had a history of untreated mental illness;
- of parents killed by children – 25.1 percent of defendants had a history of untreated mental illness; and
- of siblings killed by sibling – 17.3 percent of defendants had a history of untreated mental illness.

A 1998 MacArthur Foundation study found that people with serious brain disorders committed twice as many acts of violence in the period immediately prior to their hospitalization, when they were not taking medication, compared with the post-hospitalization period when most of them were receiving assisted treatment. Important to note, the study showed a 50 percent reduction in the rate of violence among those treated for their illness.

In addition, people with untreated mental illness living in poverty or on the street tend to be victims of crime and violence and are more prone to suicide. And, the longer a severe mental illness goes untreated, the worse it becomes and the more difficult it is to correct.

From the TAC website,

The longer individuals with serious brain disorders go untreated, the more uncertain their prospects for long-term recovery become. Recent studies have suggested that early treatment may lead to better clinical outcomes, while delaying treatment leads to worse outcomes. For example:

- A 1997 study from California (Wyatt et. al.) compared people with schizophrenia who received psychotherapy alone (89 patients) versus those who received antipsychotic medications (92 patients); those who received medications had much better outcomes three and seven years later.
- A 1998 study from England (Hopkins et. al.) revealed that delusions and hallucinations among patients suffering from psychosis increased in severity the longer treatment was withheld from the time of the initial psychotic break (51 patients were included in the study).
- A 1994 study from New York (Liebeman et. al.) showed that the longer a patient waited to receive treatment for a psychotic episode, the longer it took to get the illness into remission (70 patients were included in the study).
- A 1998 study from Italy (Tondo et. al.) demonstrated that the sooner patients were started on lithium for their manic-depressive illness, the greater their improvement became (317 patients participated in the study).

Is the stringent defense of protecting the rights of the individual worth the cost in terms of lost lives? Some lawyers and civil libertarians seem to think so.

Harvard Law School or Bellevue Psychiatric - Which is harder to Get Into?

If you are mentally ill, the answer is easy - Harvard! At least that is the opinion of D. J. Jaffe, a spokesman for the New York City Friends and Advocates of the Mentally Ill as quoted in the New York magazine "Manhattan Spirit" in 1991 and reported in Torrey. [8 70-71] Jaffe was referring to the case of a New York homeless woman named Joyce Brown and recounted in the Torrey book. It is bizarre but a perfect example of the absurdity of the system.

Ms. Brown was a mentally ill homeless woman who resided on a steam grate at E 65th Street and Second Ave in Manhattan. She urinated on the sidewalk and defecated in the gutter or on herself. At times, she tore up money passersby gave her, ran out into traffic and shouted obscenities. Many times, she was not properly dressed for the cold weather. Five times psychiatric outreach teams took her to hospital but each time she was released by psychiatrists who deemed that she was not a danger to either herself or others.

On the Diane Rehm National Public Radio show after the Virginia Tech shootings by a mentally ill man who had fallen through the cracks and should have been hospitalized before he engaged in his murderous rampage, Torrey stated somewhat sarcastically that in order to be deemed a danger to yourself or others, you have to either try to kill yourself in front of the psychiatrist or try to kill the psychiatrist. [67]

Ed Koch, the mayor at that time, saw the women and tried to have mental health professionals get her treatment. He was told that she was not deemed to be in danger or dangerous. Koch proposed new and less restrictive legislation that would make it easier to hospitalize someone. Koch referred to the civil libertarians who opposed hospitalizations as the crazies who deny people the right to treatment.

Under his new legislation, Ms. Brown was hospitalized but the New York Civil Liberties Union challenged that in court. In claiming that Ms Brown was not a threat they argued the following in her defense:

- Other New Yorkers also urinated on the sidewalk
- Defecating on oneself is not really a threat to one's health
- Running into traffic was no different than jay walking
- Tearing up money was a symbolic example of the woman's independence
- Her obscene language was no worse than what is commonly seen in movies

Judge Robert Lippman found for the Civil Liberties Union and stated that "the sight of her may improve us". By being an offense to aesthetic senses, she may spur the community to action [8][71] Upon her release, Ms. Brown was invited to appear on the Phil Donahue Show and to address a forum at Harvard Law School.

She denied any mental illness and claimed that her homelessness resulted from her not having a proper place to live. She was given a home and a temporary job. Within weeks, she was back on the streets untreated and unwell.

And the legal situation has not improved. What is commonly referred to as the Starson case in Canada makes one wonder who is ill – the diagnosed patient or the supposedly sane judges. Professor Starson, as he is continually referred to in legal documents, is neither a professor nor a man named Starson.

Scott Jeffrey Schutzman has been described as a physics savant with no formal training. He had written for scholarly journals and co-authored papers. His specialty was time measurement, anti-gravity and the theory of relativity. In 1993 according to his mother, he changed his last name to Starson because he thought he was the son of the stars. And he called himself Professor even though he was not. [68]

The courts have always referred to him as Professor Starson and the official Supreme Court of Canada citation makes reference to Professor Starson although it does provide his real name as an "aka" - also known as..

Schutzman/Starson has a long history of mental illness with at least 17 psychiatric hospitalizations. In 1998, he was detained at a forensic psychiatry facility in Ontario after being found not criminally responsible (due to a mental illness) for making death threats. He refused treatments that would have resulted in his being freed but the treating psychiatrists determined that he was not capable of making a rational treatment decision.

He appealed to the Ontario Consent and Capacity Board who sided with the psychiatrists. This board is an independent provincial tribunal whose stated mission is the fair and accessible adjudication of consent and capacity issues, balancing the rights of vulnerable individuals with public safety. Over 80 percent of it's applications involve a review of a person's involuntary status in a psychiatric facility under the Mental Health Act, or a review under the Health Care Consent Act of a person's capacity to consent to or refuse treatment.

That was appealed to the Ontario Superior Court which ruled in favor of Starson. That was then taken all the way to the Supreme Court of Canada who upheld the decisions by the lower courts and ruled that a man who calls himself a Professor, considers himself to be the son of the stars, and who has had numerous hospitalizations for psychiatric problems is capable of refusing treatment even when that refusal means that he must continue to be confined.

After almost starving himself to death in his fight to refuse treatment, Schutzman finally agreed to take medication, and in the summer of 2006, he was well enough to be moved to a minimum security forensic unit.

Eight years of legal battles and psychotic delusions could have been avoided had he been treated earlier.

As mentioned above, each jurisdiction has slightly different laws. American readers of this book can look up their own state legislation on the Treatment Advocacy Center website at:
http://www.treatmentadvocacycenter.org/LegalResources/statechart.htm

Involuntary Treatment Other Examples

There are no homeless mentally ill people in Norway. At least not according to Yale professor Thomas McGlashan who is conducting research in that country and in the state of Connecticut. In an interview with the LA Times excerpted on the Schizophrenia dot com website, McGlashan said that any mentally ill person found on the streets would be connected with an outpatient clinic and he would have a regular doctor and a nurse who visited him to ensure that he was doing well.

McGlashan added that a key difference from the North American system is that the Norwegian philosophy favors involuntary treatment rather than protecting the rights of patients who aren't well enough to know how sick they are. [69] The Norwegian government voted not to reduce beds in psychiatric hospitals until alternative services had been created for patients who were to be discharged.

In order to force hospitalization and treatment, a person must have a serious mental illness and meet at least one of the following two criteria:

- The possibility of a cure or considerable improvement will be lost if the person is not treated
- The patient represents a considerable danger to himself or to others

Patients can be admitted on a compulsory basis for up to ten days but voluntary solutions will always be tried first when possible. Compulsory treatments can be either on an inpatient or an outpatient basis. Patients have the right to appeal these orders to a supervising commission or to the courts [70]

Changes have also been made recently in the Netherlands where they removed the word serious from threat in June 2004. Previously, non consensual treatment could only be given if a person represented a serious threat to himself or others. Danger is also defined for the person with the illness (primary danger), for others (secondary danger) and for general safety (tertiary danger).

Primary danger comprises any of the following:

- that the person may take his or her own life or inflict serious self-injury
- that the person may become socially isolated
- that the person may seriously neglect him/herself
- that the behavior of the person may illicit aggressive responses from others

Secondary and tertiary dangers involve harming others physically and mentally, neglecting another person's care for whom he/she is responsible and finally a long list of potential dangers to the general safety of both people and property. [66]

The UK just approved new legislation entitled the Mental Health Act 2007 that also allows for easier detention and supervised treatment [72]

Criteria for detention includes:

- A mental disorder
- Nature or degree to warrant detention in, receive medical treatment in hospital
- In the interests of the patient's health or safety or for the protection of others

- Appropriate treatment is available (that medical treatment is available which is appropriate in the patient's case, taking into account the nature or degree of his mental disorder and all other circumstances of his case)

Medical treatment in relation to a mental disorder is to be construed as medical treatment intended to alleviate or prevent a worsening of the disorder or one or more of its symptoms or manifestations.

Supervised community treatment is called for when:

- the patient is suffering from a mental disorder of a nature or degree which makes it appropriate for them to receive medical treatment
- it is necessary for their health or safety or for the protection of other persons
- subject to their being liable to be recalled to hospital
- appropriate medical treatment is available
- the responsible clinician should be able to recall them to hospitalization
- the clinician should consider the risks that the patient might comply with community treatment and not deteriorate.

If legislation like those in Norway, the Netherlands and the UK had been in place in North America then many of the tragedies that occur on a regular basis might not happen. The two examples cited above, that of Ms Brown and the self proclaimed professor would both have met the criteria for hospitalization and treatment in Norway, the Netherlands and the UK.

CHAPTER SIX – TREATMENT STRATEGIES

Consensus Guidelines

Almost all diseases and medical problems have what are called treatment or consensus guidelines and treatment algorithms. Experts in a particular field look at all the evidence from research and determine the appropriate methods for evaluating patients and the best way to treat them.

That is the case in psychiatry and both the Canadian Psychiatric Association [73] and the American Psychiatric Association [74] have guidelines for the appropriate treatment of schizophrenia. Needless to say, they are pretty similar since both are based on the current scientific literature. The Canadian Psychiatric Association worked with the Schizophrenia Society of Canada to translate their guidelines into language that lay people can understand [75] If you have a loved one with schizophrenia then this is a very valuable resource. You can check to see if the doctors are following the best methods in treating. Not surprisingly, there sometimes is a gap between best practices and reality.

Treatment varies depending upon the stage of the disease. Schizophrenia is divided into first episode and/or acute phase, stabilization phase and the stable or chronic state. First episode psychosis and the acute phase are similar in that they are characterized by active symptoms that need to be diagnosed and treated. Stabilization occurs after treatment when the symptoms have become less acute while chronic refers to the period when the acute symptoms are being managed. The person may still have difficulty coping with every day life and there is always the danger of regressing back into the acute stage.

The mainstay of treatment is pharmacotherapy – drugs. It is very rare for anyone to be able to manage their illness without drugs and is is estimated that 90% of people will relapse within one year of stopping medication.

Unfortunately, depression is a problem with people who are newly diagnosed. This is often the result of their realization that their dreams and hopes for the future may never be realized. That they have a chronic illness. This, combined with only partial recovery, results in an estimated 4 to 6 out of every 10 people diagnosed with schizophrenia attempting suicide. Many, unfortunately, succeed, and about 5 to 10% of people with schizophrenia die by suicide.

The common analogy that is used for treatment is that people with schizophrenia, like diabetics or epileptics, need their medications. The Canadian Psychiatric Association provides the following as its recommendations.

- Antipsychotic medications are needed for nearly all patients experiencing an acute relapse. The choice of medication should be tailored according to what is happening with the patient.
- In first-episode psychosis, dosages should be started in the lower half of the treatment range.
- Maintenance of medication is needed to avoid relapse in the stabilization and stable phases.
- Antipsychotic medication for the treatment of a first-episode psychosis should be continued for a minimum of one year following first recovery of

symptoms and indefinitely for multi-episode schizophrenia.

- Long-acting injectable antipsychotic medication should be considered for people who do not follow their treatment program consistently or who have trouble taking oral medication regularly.
- Clozapine may be indicated for people who have tried two or more other antipsychotics without sufficient improvement in positive symptoms, have intolerable side effects or unremitting aggressive or suicidal behavior.
- A major depressive episode during the stable phase of schizophrenia may indicate the need for a trial of an antidepressant.

Treatment, however, should involve more than just prescription drugs. What is called psychosocial interventions are also needed to go along with the pharmaceuticals. These strategies will help improve clinical symptoms, functional abilities and quality of life. They include education about the disease, skills and education training, financial, housing and job support, diet, exercise and nutrition counseling, cognitive therapy, and family planning.

The delivery of service should be comprehensive and include physical care by a family doctor, 24 hour crisis care, in-patient accessibility, and case management services.

All this is the ideal, and those are the services you should demand for your relative or for yourself. How many with schizophrenia actually receive this level of care in either the US or Canada is a matter for conjecture. Given that deinstitutionalization took place without proper community supports in place and the number of people with serious

122

mental illness amongst the homeless and/or in jail, the suspicion is: not many.

First Episode Early Intervention

In most areas of medicine, early detection is the goal. The success rate for cancer is often better if the cancer is detected early and treated before it gains a foothold or begins to spread. This concept is starting to become accepted in schizophrenia as well. In a 2005 Australian Broadcasting Corporation interview, Dr. Patrick McGorry said "just as in any other part of medicine or health care, early diagnosis is a much more effective and cost effective way to treat people. That's well established in cancer, heart disease, diabetes and anywhere else. It's been a difficult struggle to get that accepted in psychiatry but now there's increasing evidence – particularly for psychotic disorders, but also for other kinds of potentially severe mental illnesses – that the same principle applies" [76]

Dr. McGorry is one of the world's leading experts in early intervention. Efforts are now being made in an increasing number of clinics throughout the world to identify as early as possible behavior that might lead to schizophrenia and to treat it. The hope is that someday there might be a physical test such as a blood test combined with observed behavior and genetic evaluations that will predict the onset of schizophrenia. The disease will then be able to be treated to prevent a full blown case.

The work of the PRIME clinic and the concept of the prodromol symptoms of schizophrenia was discussed in chapter 3. Many sites throughout the world are attempting to pick up on potential schizophrenia symptoms at an early stage and these are known as first episode clinics. The importance of this approach is mentioned in the guidelines but we do not have enough clinics to provide assessment for those at risk or treatment for those who need it. Many in the community – teachers, social workers, doctors, parents, etc – are usually not aware of the warning signs.

The Canadian Guidelines make reference to the ultra high-risk mental state which they define as either the onset of attenuated psychotic symptoms not reaching threshold for psychosis or brief intermittent psychotic symptoms lasting less than seven days or a combination of a trait (positive family history of psychosis in first degree relatives) and a significant decline in global functioning in the previous year. While that may be a mouthful, they state that 30% to 40% of the people who meet these criteria will go on to develop full blown psychosis within the year.

No treatment can yet be recommended for those who might go on to become sick but preliminary data does exist to suggest that low and/or medium doses of antipsychotic medication may reduce the chance of conversion to psychosis or at least reduce the severity of the symptoms and improve functioning. A similar finding was demonstrated when cognitive behavioral training was used in place of drugs.

While the ultimate aim of early detection is true primary prevention, according to a document put out by NAMI in 1997 [77], and is designed to eliminate the vulnerability to schizophrenia or to block its expression developmentally, we are a long way from it. One of the earliest programs designed to be a comprehensive model of care for those aged 16 to 25 and to delay the time period between onset and treatment to prevent damage was the Early Psychosis Prevention and Intervention Centre (EPPIC) in Melbourne

Australia. This is the clinic established by Dr. McGorry quoted above.

This model program has a mobile assessment team that provides information and support and offers psychotherapy to help prevent the depression, anxiety, demoralization and lowered self esteem associated with a psychotic episode. It promotes the use of low doses of medications when required as they have been found to be effective in these cases. Outpatient case managers work with families to help reduce relapse.

More recently, the National Institute for Mental Illness in England summed up the services that currently exist for early intervention as "too little and too late". [78] They stated:

- Those with a first episode experience delays in recognition and treatment of 1-2 years by which time the level of illness may well be severe
- Excessive delay is a significant contributor to poor response to treatment, recovery and long term outcome
- Most are hospitalized initially in crisis and often with police involvement
- There are complaints about the lack of practical help and education about psychosis while the clinical attention focuses on treatment issues and neglects personal adaptation, functional recovery, relapse prevention and the needs of the caregivers
- Because of coercive early experiences and stigma about mental illness, 50% of these young people are lost to follow up within 12 months but they often reappear later in crisis during a relapse
- More than half will relapse within 18 months and with each relapse the speed and quality of remission will be progressively impaired. At the same time, the risk

of further relapse and persisting symptoms increases.

- By five years, the majority (55%)of patients will be unable to achieve remission from their episodes of psychosis.

Think of how many lives could be improved and how many young people could be saved from homelessness, incarceration, and misery if only we had more clinics. Of course, part of the problem is stigma and the unwillingness of those who are becoming ill to admit that they might be sick. These are issues that must be dealt with by our society.

Assertive Community Treatment (ACT)

The best definition of ACT comes from the website for the Ontario based organization, the Coalition for Appropriate Care and Treatment (CFACT).[79] That is ACT teams provide comprehensive, integrated treatment, rehabilitation and support to individuals with serious mental illness who require intensive community mental health care services. The ACT model, developed in Wisconsin in 1972, has been disseminated internationally and is the most rigorously researched evidence-based best practice in community mental health. More than 30 years of peer reviewed research has demonstrated that individuals who receive ACT are less likely to be hospitalized and more likely to have stable housing than those who receive less intensive services.

The team provides services to individuals with complex, treatment refractory mental illnesses with major psychotic symptoms who have not benefited from less intensive services as demonstrated by frequent relapse and hospitalization. The ACT program provides highly individualized multi-disciplinary services directly to individuals in their homes and community environments 24 hours a day, 7 days a week, 365 days a year.

It's intent is to provide:

- psychiatric treatment, medication services, individual therapy, crisis intervention, and substance abuse services,
- rehabilitation, education, vocational, recreational services, skill teaching, and activities of daily living and
- support (family services, medical/dental services, housing support, transportation, criminal justice services and advocacy)

An evaluation of the program in Ontario in 2002-2003 found the following results:

- Average per client hospital bed day reductions of 67% to 83% had been achieved 1 year through 4 years post-ACT.
  (Actual use = 86 days 1-year pre-ACT, down to 28 days 1-year post-ACT, to 15 days 4 years post-ACT.)
- Average per client bed cost was reduced from $41,796 to $13,608 after 1 year of ACT services and $7,290 after 4 years.
- Total projected bed cost reduction for 2,887 Ontario ACT clients was $82,000,000*
  (* does not include the cost of ACT care)
- Results show that 71% more clients are living in a home of their own after ACT.

- 91% of the target population is receiving novel anti-psychotic medication.
- 91% of clients are satisfied or very satisfied with services from the ACT team.
- 94% of family members are satisfied or very satisfied with ACT services.

Mandated Outpatient Treatments (MOT)

MOT is a generic term referring to community treatment orders (CTOs), court ordered outpatient committal (available in most jurisdictions in the US), conditional leave from hospital (available in many Canadian provinces), and guardianship legislation which is also available in many Canadian provinces. [80]

CTO is a legal provision whereby a doctor can require a person with a mental illness to follow a course of treatment while living in the community. That person must meet certain stringent criteria. The rational for CTOs is that deinstitutionalization results in people being released into the community who do not have sufficient insight into their illness to understand that they need treatment. Those who support CTOs believe that society has a duty to ensure that these individuals receive appropriate care and treatment. Opponents object to the coercive nature of the CTOs and fear that they will have unanticipated consequences. They believe they will be overused and that there are viable alternatives to this coercion.

Those who oppose compulsory treatment and those who support it can find support from the philosopher John Stuart Mill in his thesis "On Liberty". Those who oppose compulsory treatment refer to Mill's statement that "the only purpose for which power can be rightfully exercised over any member of a civilized community, against his will, is to prevent harm to others. His own good, either physical or moral, is not sufficient warrant." Of course, when Mill wrote this, there were very few suitable medical treatments for anything let alone mental disorders.

However, Dr. Richard O'Reilly who does support CTOs points out in his paper that in the very next paragraph Mill says "Those who are still in a state to require being taken care of by others must be protected against their own actions as well as against personal injury." Therein, he says, lies the source of conflict between the deontologists and the utilitarians. Deontologists believe that some actions are wrong regardless of the consequences and, in this debate, they feel that forced treatment is wrong regardless. Deontologists propose that individual autonomy is absolute and must be respected in all circumstances, whereas utilitarians believe that the negative consequences of allowing patients suffering from psychosis freedom of choice should, in some cases, limit that choice.

Outcome research into the effectiveness of CTOs is clouded, equivocal and controversial. Most of the studies have used hospital stay as the main outcome measure of the research but O'Reilly argues that this is not an appropriate measure. Some patients, he argues, may actually benefit from hospital stays which they might not have agreed to without the order in place.

The studies done have been consistent in demonstrating that patients are more likely to follow up with mental health services as a result of the CTO. A study in North Carolina found that CTO patients were less likely to be victimized while other studies found that CTO patients were less likely to be violent. A five year evaluation of Kendra's Law in New York State showed that there were increases in involvement with services, adherence to medication, and improvements in self care activities of daily living. There were decreases in substance abuse, assaultive, anti-social and self harm behavior, hospitalization rates, homelessness, arrest and incarceration.

A study recently published on CTOs in Toronto found that they helped to assist people who normally would refuse treatment to continue with mental health services. [81]

One very illustrative example is of a woman who was a top student but, when untreated, stands on street corners shouting invectives at strangers. When treated, she works as an assistant on film productions. She is currently working and is on a CTO.

Another strategy is to use what is called an advance directive. The ill individual can either appoint someone to act on his/her behalf when and if they become ill again. This proxy decision maker ensures the treatment that the person wants is given. A Ulysses contract is one in which the individual sets out that force may be used to ensure treatment compliance. In place of a proxy, the individual can simply outline the types of treatments that are acceptable. This is similar to what is commonly referred to as a living will for the elderly or those with terminal illnesses. Needless to say, it requires considerable insight into the illness on the part of the person with schizophrenia when they are at a very young age.

According to an article on the topic in the Washington Post, [82] advance directives give someone the opportunity to control their treatments when they are ill and incapable. In the example they use, a woman who had a directive in place had specified they if she became ill then she was to be given zyprexa rather than haldol.

About 25 states allow for these directives which require two witnesses and notarization in order to become legal. In some states, patients are allowed to revoke the orders even when they are in psychotic states and not competent. Some fear that having an irrevocable clause in an advanced directive would be the same as coercive treatment.

Psychiatrists in Blue

It is a sad reflection on the state of our treatment programs that very often the front line mental health care workers are police officers. Often, and in the experiences of this writer and many others, they provide as compassionate, and sometimes more, care than the trained mental health workers. The police are not initially trained to provide care and treatment but that is changing because of reality. In fact, the title of this section is taken from the name for an annual conference held in Canada since 2002.

The Canadian conference is organized by the Canadian National Committee for Police/Mental Health Liaison. The primary goal of the organization is to ensure that individuals who suffer from mental illnesses are not "criminalized" inappropriately but rather are directed toward the system which is most appropriate for them in their circumstances. It may be that this means entry into the criminal justice system if indeed a crime has been committed—but equally, it may mean that they are directed to the mental health system, or—if it is their choice and they do not represent a danger—no system at all. Obvious as this goal may be, it has often fallen to police departments in recent years to take the lead role in directing these individuals to services. Lack of easily accessible community mental health services combined with the comfortable public expectation that the police fix all things means that calls to assist a person with a mental illness who appears to be in trouble go to the police. [83]

This is not something that is unique to Canada. One of the keynote speakers at the above conference was a specialist from Australia. In an article in Catalyst put out by the Treatment Advocacy Center, Donald F. Eslinger wrote an article entitled "The Sheriff as Advocate". Eslinger is sheriff of Seminole County in Florida and he wrote "Sheriffs are not medical professionals. And yet, my deputies are increasingly called on to handle dangerous situations involving people with untreated severe mental illnesses. This situation has become a public safety concern for our officers and the citizens we are charged to protect." [84]

An example of the involvement of the police with the seriously mentally ill was demonstrated in a four year longitudinal study between 1998 and 2001 in the medium sized Canadian city of London, Ontario. [85] This study found that there was an increase in the time spent by police with mentally ill people and for which they are largely untrained. Most of these contacts are for non violent and nuisance type complaints. The police chief commented that these contacts could be better handled by improved community mental health supports.

In 2001, the officers spent more than twice the number of hours on mentally ill people than they did in 1998 and cost the police $2.4 million out of their total budget of $43 million. That money could have provided considerable community services.

A More Ideal System?

In many jurisdictions, the system for treating those with serious mental illnesses is a non system. While there are some good programs in some areas, overall we do not provide adequate, rational, evidence based, comprehensive services for people with serious mental illnesses. Let's face it. If we did, then most jurisdictions would not have so many with serious mental illness in jail, homeless or living in despair.

As the Scientist magazine pointed out in its special issue, "some people with schizophrenia can, with appropriate support, hold down jobs and even succeed in demanding careers, but most find themselves unable to work and services to help get people with schizophrenia into the workforce are scarce. One 2006 study of more than 1,400 people with schizophrenia, average age 41, found that just 14.5% were employed in the mainstream workforce. That compares to 80.9% employment of US men and women aged 35-44....." [58]

The employment rate for people with schizophrenia in Germany is double at about 30% based on a survey done in Germany, France and the UK. [86] In fact, the highest proportion of people with schizophrenia supporting themselves entirely through work was in Germany. The authors of the study noted that many with mental illness are isolated and excluded from society. Not being allowed to work is a factor that can contribute to this problem.

Data on work is not available for the Netherlands and that country was not included in the study but their system seems to be a model that we should look at. Unlike most other countries, the Dutch had "no distinct period of deinstitutionalization or transinstitutionalization of mental health care. Rather, the Dutch government expects local mental health services to reform their joint service provision without forceful measures like cutting budgets of large mental hospitals" [87]

In the Netherlands, the first effort to reduce inpatient care of patients was not to cut budgets as was done in places like North America, Italy, Germany and the UK but to strengthen outpatient care. Small specialized providers of outpatient care were integrated into regional institutes for ambulatory care (RIAGGs). Their role was to be an alternative to hospitals.

In the 1980s, focus then shifted from these RIAGGs to other alternatives to hospital for those with long term needs. The provision of day treatment, sheltered residences and assertive home treatment was left to the private not for profits who provide almost all of these services. The government role was to support local experiments and to eliminate barriers to change.

Rather than forcing innovation by cutting budgets, the Dutch stimulated change and thus the deinstitutionalization process was much slower there than in other countries. However, the result has been that the average person spends fewer days a year in hospital while intensive community based care has increased considerably.

In 1955, there were 28,000 psychiatric beds in that country but by 1996 the number of beds was reduced to 22,885. [88] Two thirds of those beds are for patients who have been hospitalized for more than one year. A little over a third of these long term beds are actually staffed group homes connected to the hospitals. Partial hospitalization has also been developed in the past few years as an alternative to full time stay.

There are also sheltered living accommodations in the community that housed over 5500 patients in 1998. These group homes provide support for an additional 2500 people who live independently. Homeless psychiatric people are provided for in additional residential settings numbering 1400 in 1998.

Day care, walk in and rehab centers also exist for those with serious mental illness. For 1998, there were 131 such places that had been established over the previous 15 years as deinstitutionalization occurred. Each place provides service to about 150 users and 16,000 people use these centers annually.

The country also has active consumer and family organizations that are involved in care. In 1964, a group called Pandora was established to help reduce the stigma of mental illness and help rehabilitate. The League of Clients was founded in 1971 by relatives and professionals but this later evolved into a client or user organization. It's focus was advocacy and empowerment and it was instrumental in the establishment of a patient confidential counselor (PVP) in 1981. The PVP is available for all inpatients to report on problems during hospital stays.

In 1980, the Foundation of Patient Councils (LPR) was formed nationally and now has a large professional office staff. Their main goal is to ensure patient rights and to be involved in all aspects of decision making in psychiatry and mental health. In that same decade, a number of family organizations were also established such as Ypsilon which was made up of family members of those with psychoses.

In 1996, legislation was passed to allow client councils to be active participants and advisors in the development, organization and quality of services offered. The LPR developed a quality assurance instrument for clients to audit services provided. Family organizations are also recognized by both the government and mental health care services as an independent and important contributor to services. Families have family councils in 30 mental hospitals in the country.

CHAPTER SEVEN – STIGMA

Introduction

Probably the biggest problem faced by most people with serious mental illnesses, and particularly those with schizophrenia, is stigma. It is bad enough to have a serious chronic illness yourself or to see a loved one with a serious chronic illness but that is made even worse by stigma. The image that we see in the media and in society is often wrong, demeaning and discriminatory.

Some progress is being made and there is a greater understanding of diseases like depression, obsessive compulsive disorder and even bipolar but that enlightenment is only partial as we shall see and hardly extends into schizophrenia at all. The negative and incorrect views held about schizophrenia (even in the medical community) make it difficult for young people to seek help or to accept a diagnosis and the help associated with that. It makes it difficult for the families who not only must contend with having a sick child but who get little or no help or sympathy from either family or friends.

Imagine being a parent of someone with schizophrenia and being in a theater enjoying Billy Crystal's one man show "700 Sundays" and listening to him tell of his mother's final illness and death. Suddenly, he throws in a joke about people with schizophrenia that is based on a totally incorrect premise of what the disease really is. [89] And the audience laughs. Surely Crystal is not so desperate for laughs that he must demean people with schizophrenia but that is considered acceptable. And, he is not alone.

Nancy Andreason suggests that one very big reason for stigma is the "not in my backyard or NIMBY syndrome". [36] She says that most of us who are healthy or wealthy do not enjoy being confronted by suffering, poverty or disfigurement. In order to shelter ourselves from these sorts, we always put up institutions called poorhouses, madhouses, orphanages and jails. These unfortunates could be hidden away. While it may not have been right to mix together people like criminals, the physically disfigured, those with mental retardation, schizophrenics and the poor, we did so out of social convenience. When these people are grouped together and hidden from view, it becomes easy to see that people have become confused and associate bad with mad.

In the Media

If anyone doubts the extent of stigma in society, simply visit the National Alliance for the Mentally ill anti-stigma archives and the advocacy via stigmabusters website to get a sampling of the extent of the problem. NAMI stigmabusters (taken from their website) is a network of dedicated advocates across the US and around the world who seek to fight inaccurate and hurtful representations of mental illness.

Whether these images are found in TV, film, print, or other media, StigmaBusters speak out and challenge stereotypes. They seek to educate society about the reality of mental illness and the courageous struggles faced by consumers and families every day. StigmaBusters' goal is to break down the barriers of ignorance, prejudice, or unfair discrimination by promoting education, understanding, and respect.

The number of examples of bad taste and stigma-encouraging activities are numerous but one of many is the 2000 Jim Carrey film "Me Myself and Irene" which helps to perpetuate the incorrect view that schizophrenia is multiple personalities. NAMI launched a publicity campaign with the message that it is not acceptable to make fun of people with mental illness. As the result of the letter writing, the advertising campaign for the film was changed.

20th Century Fox newspaper ads eliminated the split head of Jim Carrey with the statement "From Gentle to Mental" and replaced it with the visual of his full laughing face with adjectives describing his comedic antics and stunts in the movie. His media interviews later switched to a focus on his risky stunts, with accompanying movie clips. NAMI reported that "unfortunately, Jim Carrey declined to participate in a NAMI public service announcement to educate the public about the true nature of mental illnesses"

In 2004, Jive Records released a debut solo album by JC Chasez, who once sang in the band N'Sync. The title of the album is "Schizophrenic." On the cover, along with promotional advertisements, is the image of a person strapped in a straitjacket.

And even the popular TV psychologist propelled to fame by Oprah is not immune from perpetuating myths about mental illness. Here is the NAMI complaint about Dr. Phil from a 2004 show that he did:

NAMI has charged CBS TV with gross irresponsibility for its September 22 broadcast of the "Dr. Phil Primetime Special: Family First," in which the so-called pop psychologist not only "blamed parents first," but may have endangered the lives of children with severe mental illnesses.

"Not only did the show represent a breach of professional ethics, but also, in the opinion of many, malpractice", declared NAMI executive director Michael J. Fitzpatrick, in a letter to CBS Chairman & CEO Leslie Moonves, co-signed by Suzanne Vogel-Scibilia, MD, a child psychiatrist who chairs the Child & Adolescent Policy Subcommittee of NAMI's national board.

The show was especially troubling because the child's behavior may have suggested symptoms of bipolar disorder, requiring treatment vastly different from a father being admonished to spend more time with his son to 'go fishing.'

"Blaming the family undermines all recent understanding of the biological basis of brain disorders and is not only insensitive, but also hinders a family or individual from seeking comprehensive treatment," NAMI warned.

In the Military

A more recent example of total ignorance involves the US military. Post traumatic stress disorder (PTSD) is a recognized psychiatric condition. According to the online medical website medicinenet.com, PTSD is an emotional illness that develops as a result of a terribly frightening, life-threatening, or otherwise highly unsafe experience. PTSD sufferers re-experience the traumatic event or events in some way, tend to avoid places, people, or other things that remind them of the event (avoidance), and are exquisitely sensitive to normal life experiences (hyperarousal).

It's formal diagnosis only goes back to 1980 but it was first recognized during the American Civil War as "soldiers heart". During World War I, it was called battle fatigue; during the second war it was gross stress reaction and then, for Vietnam, post-Vietnam syndrome. It has also been called shell shock.

It's validity as a consequence of battle is well recognized and it has been further legitimized by Canadian general Romeo Dallaire. General Dallaire left the Canadian Forces because of his PTSD in 2000 and has spoken a great deal about the problem. He had led the UN mission to Rwanda during the slaughter of tens of thousands of people and was unable to convince the UN to send reinforcements or to stop the killing of women and children.

Unfortunately, views have not improved during the Iraq war. According to the Washington Post, 1st Lt Elizabeth Whiteside is facing court martial and life imprisonment for attempting suicide and thus endangering the life of another soldier. [90] Military psychiatrists at Walter Reed Army Hospital diagnosed her with a severe mental disorder possibly triggered by the stress of war. Whiteside served as a platoon leader in a Medical Company at a prisoner camp near Baghdad International Airport. It was there that she attempted suicide.

Despite the psychiatric diagnosis, her superior officers considered her mental illness as an excuse for criminal conduct based on government records obtained by the Washington Post. The military prosecutor informed her defense lawyer about the risk of using "a psychobabble" defense.

While the Pentagon has spent hundreds of millions of dollars on new research and to care for soldiers with PTSD, that thinking has not filtered down to the ranks. The Post stated that mental health issues are still based on the ad

141

hoc judgment of combat hardened officers "whose understanding of mental illness is vague or misinformed".

But then, it would seem that the new spending is also not being reflected in simple supports for wounded soldiers. Family members of soldiers recovering from physical wounds at Walter Reed are provided with free lodging and a per diem so that they can be near to and support their loved ones. Families of those with psychiatric patients usually have to pay their own way.

In its letter of support for Lt Whiteside and its plea for greater understanding of PTSD, NAMI reminded the Army of an infamous incident during the Second World War when General Patton publicly slapped a shell shocked soldier. But then, that was an improvement on the British and Commonwealth army during the first war who executed deserters by firing squad. "Many of the men executed had previous records of being treated for shell shock, in some cases three or four times, and many of them tried to use that to explain their actions. Each time they would be admitted to a forward hospital for a week or two and then released back to full duty". [91]

But the British have not advanced all that much since the "first great war" and are still treating their shell shock troops badly and just as badly as the Americans. Take for example the case of Lance Corporal James Piotrowski of the Irish Guard. In April 2006, he was sentenced to seven years and four months in prison when the court rejected his defense of PTSD. [92]

The military judge stated that "given the psychiatric reports we have read, the court regards you as a dangerous offender" and he then went on to say that if he had the power he would sentence him to an indeterminate sentence. The 21 year old had joined the military at age 18 and was named top recruit. He was in the front line of the Iraq invasion in 2003 but on his return to England he "quickly went off the rails" and had continual flashbacks.

As he always had a weapon with him in Iraq, he felt that he needed one at home in order to feel safe and stole at least one automatic weapon from the military barracks. Military police found it in pieces under his bed. His defense was PTSD but that was rejected by the military tribunal. An army doctor testified that he "certainly describes a number of post traumatic symptoms but I am not convinced he fulfills the full criteria for PTSD".

A leading specialist in combat stress testified "I have seen many ex-servicemen suffering similar conditions who feel naked and apprehensive without some weapon on their person or within access. This is the process underlying the possession of the rifle in this case".

His mother can be seen describing the event on Britain's channel four alternative Christmas message 2007 on the French equivalent of Youtube. The URL is http://www.dailymotion.com/oddball71/video/x3v1ex_alterna tive-christmas-message-2007_news

A British Example

A 2007 survey report from the Priory Group at the Priory Hospital in Roehampton England described the extent of stigma that exists in that country towards those with mental illness. [26] The report is called "Crying Shame" and, in the introduction, psychiatrist Natasha Bijlani stated:

- A shocking 72% of adults in Great Britain believe that there is a stigma associated with having a mental illness and describe people with mental illness as unpredictable (79%), dangerous (50%) and scary (49%).
- Less than half (45%) of the adult population think that people with long-term mental illnesses are able to lead independent, fulfilled lives.
- Over half of British adults (52%) agree that being diagnosed with a serious mental illness and being diagnosed with cancer are as bad as each other and
- 57% believe that all aspects of their lives would be negatively affected if they were diagnosed with a mental illness.
- Most damningly, 77% of adults state that the media does not do a good job in educating people about mental illness and
- 76% say that the media does not do a good job in de-stigmatising mental illness.

The report states that people with mental illness experience stigma in the following ways:

- Being seen as different.
- Being regarded as socially unacceptable.
- Being alienated.
- Being discriminated against.
- Being verbally abused and harassed.
- Worrying too much about what other people will say.
- Being the subject of a set of unreasonable generalizations that may be passed from generation to generation.

- Being the subject of a range of negative views and perceptions by other people (for instance, that we are always 'down' and unhappy).
- Being seen as the unknown quantity – as another species.
- Being a group that other people do not know how to talk to or act with.
- Not being normal.
- Feeling ashamed and weak because we cannot cope.
- Being avoided.
- Being seen as failures and as weak.
- Being seen as unpredictable.
- Not being seen as part of social conversations. People often don't speak about illness, as the intensity of emotion is not acceptable to them.
- Being seen as 'mad' or 'nuts'.
- Being labelled and stereotyped and defined by our illness.
- Not being understood.

A very insightful comment made in the report is that as the result of stigma "the world often shrinks to a miniscule landscape for many people with mental illness: instead of engaging with a variety of people in their broader community, their community reduces down to the mental health community – a coterie of patients, carers, social workers and other healthcare providers."

In the Medical Profession

It is sad but often people with serious mental illnesses face discrimination from those who should know better. As part of a project for the World Psychiatric Association's global campaign to fight stigma and discrimination, Dr Heather Stuart, a psychologist, and Dr. Julio Arboleda-Florez, a psychiatrist, conducted a survey in Alberta, Canada. The survey was designed to find out about attitudes of the public towards those with schizophrenia.

Their findings, published in the Canadian Journal of Psychiatry in April 2001 had some surprising results. [93] Most people were relatively well informed and progressive in their understanding of schizophrenia and its treatment. However, it was found that those who work with the mentally ill were not as tolerant as would be expected from their education and choice of work.

The authors stated that "these finding support the perception of those with schizophrenia that their most stigmatizing experiences occur within the mental health provider community in which they have their most frequent contacts".

This stigmatization of people with serious mental illnesses was the subject of a paper presented at the Royal College of Psychiatrists Annual Meeting in 2007 in Edinburgh. Drs Alex Mitchell and Darren Malone looked at medical screening of psychiatric patients for cholesterol, high blood pressure, diabetes, osteoporosis, HIV and cervical and breast cancer and treatment for diabetes, cardiovascular disease, HIV and cancer care. Elevated cholesterol and diabetes are two common side effects of antipsychotic medication so one would expect physicians to be more vigilant about screening for this problem in patients on those drugs.

Of 14 studies that evaluated health screening, 12 suggested that psychiatric patients received inferior quality of care. Of the 23 studies comparing care for patients with and without mental illness, 14 suggested poor quality of care when it came to recommending drug treatment, diagnostic and investigative procedures and surgical interventions.

Dr. Mitchell, a psychiatrist, made these two very damning statements.

"People who are mentally ill sometimes don't seek screening, but the most powerful reason is that once the medical team knows a patient has psychiatric problems, they give them poorer quality of care"

"Doctors don't like dealing with patients with psychiatric problems. They view them as different and they spend less time with them. They don't offer the patients the same intensity of investigations as the non mentally-ill patient. It's prejudicial treatment." [94]

And it is that prejudicial treatment that may have led to the death of a 40 year old man with schizophrenia in Hamilton, Ontario.

Rusty Potter died in July of 2002 in the waiting room of the emergency department at St. Joseph's Health Centre. Suffering with asthma, he had gone to the ER with pneumonia. St. Joseph's is also home to the local emergency psychiatric unit and staff probably recognized his home address as that of a group home for psychiatric patients run by the Canadian Mental Health Association. He was also a volunteer at the hospital.

Unfortunately, the ER nurses did not realize that he was in medical distress even though he was struggling to breathe. One of the nurses handed him a paper bag to breathe into which is a common strategy for those having a panic attack. It was not a panic attack but a combination of his asthma and his pneumonia. Rusty collapsed and died in the waiting room.

Gwen Davidson, the psychiatric patient advocate who knew Rusty, said in a letter to the Hamilton Spectator that "unfortunately, his death reinforces the concern that persons with mental illness do not obtain appropriate medical treatment. All too often, our clients don't get access to medical services or their concerns go unrecognized because the symptoms are viewed as 'part of their illness' or that they are 'attention seeking' by asking for help". [95,96]

Journalist/physician Dr. Miriam Shuchman who teaches medical ethics at the State University of New York at Buffalo and the University of Toronto wrote about the case in the Toronto Globe and Mail. She stated that "people with chronic mental illness are at higher risk for medical illnesses than the general population. They need general medical care. Yet, they are less likely to be treated for medical problems than the next person. Mental illness leads to cognitive difficulties that can prevent a patient from seeking medical care. When they do go to a doctor's office or an emergency room, the staff may be uncomfortable treating them." [97]

On this topic, the final word should go to Dr. Bijlani, the author of the British report referred to above. She said "some doctors are still prejudiced against patients with mental illness and I have been told, 'you work with loonies.' If one doctor can say this to another, what hope can we hold out for the rest of society?"

CHAPTER EIGHT – THE NAYSAYERS

I f you've persevered to this point in the book, you realize that schizophrenia and other serious mental illnesses have their base in physical changes in the brain and that the cause is highly complex and still not fully understood. Treatment involves drug therapy in almost all cases but that is imperfect by itself. Aside from side effects that are often unavoidable for almost any illness where drugs are used, the drugs are still imperfect. Treatment needs to be supplemented with other modalities. These include, support, psychosocial rehabilitation, cognitive behavior therapy and other strategies.

Despite the success with drug therapy, there are groups who actively oppose this. In fact, this author will be accused of being in the pay of the big pharmaceutical companies for writing this book. It has already happened because of other work done by this author. Telling people with schizophrenia that they should not take their medications is like telling an epileptic to not take anti-seizure medication or a type I diabetic who is insulin dependent not to take insulin.

There are three groups in society who are actively opposed to drug use. The first are the Scientologists.

Scientology

The most visible spokesperson for Scientology is actor Tom Cruise who created a furor on the NBC Today show by berating Brooke Shields for taking antidepressants for her post partum depression. Cruise insisted that the host, Matt Lauer, did not know the history of psychiatry while he, Cruise, did.

Mr. Cruise's performance resulted in the president of the National Coalition of Human Rights Activists, David Rice, holding a press conference and publicly censuring Cruise. Rice stated that "when a paying customer of a flying saucer cult starts giving medical advice people need to question the authority, if not sanity, of the speaker" [98]

What people may not realize, the press release stated, is that Scientology teaches as a scientific fact that aliens from outer space created the entire mental health care profession on earth in order to enslave humanity. Founder L Ron Hubbard, a science fiction writer who was himself diagnosed with schizophrenia in the late 1940s, claimed that space alien psychiatrists created pain, sex and death and that modern mental health care professionals are controlled and manipulated by these space aliens.

In 1969, the Scientologists created the Citizens Commission on Human Rights to "investigate and expose psychiatric violations of human rights" [99] Their website claims that no mental diseases have ever been proven to medically exist and they claim that psychiatry kills and is linked with Naziism, apartheid and school violence. The group has promoted legislation in Florida, Utah and New Hampshire that seek to discredit psychiatry and drug therapies especially for kids.

At the end of 2007, the German government which has never recognized scientology as a religion, declared that it is unconstitutional. This move clears the way for a possible ban in future. [100]

The Consumer Survivor Movement

This phenomenon was briefly touched upon in the introduction and is described in considerable detail by psychiatrist/author Sally Satel in her excellent book, "P.C. MD". [101] PC stands for politically correct and her chapter on this phenomenon is called "Inmates Take Over the Asylum". She points out that she does not disagree that psychiatric patients have been treated insensitively and even maltreated. She would, she says, work with consumer survivors to help weed out incompetents and to improve the system if that is what they stood for. Unfortunately, they wish to run the system, deny the use of drugs and to prevent people from getting proper treatment when they need to be treated without consent.

Radical consumer survivors, she says, despite their fringe rhetoric and modest numbers (possibly in the hundreds only), "have infiltrated the mental health system in ways that are truly destructive".

The Center for Mental Health Services (CMHS), is one very active group that holds an annual conference called Alternatives. At one conference, a psychologist by the name of Al Siebert gave a talk on schizophrenia called "Successful Schizophrenia – The Survivor Personality". The program stated that this would be a talk on how schizophrenia is a healthy, valid, desirable condition and not a disorder. He claimed that it has never been proven to be an illness or a disease.

While these activists often claim to have been once diagnosed as schizophrenic themselves Satel, as have other psychiatrists, points out that no one with schizophrenia would have the focus, organizational ability or stamina to carry on with the campaigns that they carry on unless, of course, they were receiving treatment.

Satel is also critical of mental health administrators who she says seem willing to sacrifice the needs of those with the most severe illnesses to political correctness and to the expediency of placating the vocal and annoying consumer-survivor lobby. By supporting them or by doing nothing when they are given funding or administrative control, these administrators are promoting a movement that has had disastrous consequences for people with severe psychiatric illness.

Administrators at the psychiatric hospital near this author's home paid one of the gurus of this movement to hold a day long workshop with their staff. The editorial that this author wrote for the schizophrenia dot com website after attending the workshop is presented below. It was posted on May 27, 2005 and is still on the website [102]

Dr. Daniel Fisher, a psychiatrist who suffers from schizophrenia and who heads the National Empowerment Center, told the audience at his recovery workshop in Hamilton, Ontario that when he first entered psychiatry he found that his ideas ran counter to the newly emerging physiological theories of mental illness. "They were all jumping on the brain and I was jumping off" he said.

While science has made considerable progress in defining the changes in the brain of people with serious mental illness, Fisher continues to espouse controversial views to the point where a number of participants at the Hamilton workshop that I talked to were angered. One family member told me that she could hardly wait to get out she was so outraged by his comments that serious mental illness is an emotional problem and that people do not hear voices they just have loud thoughts.

Others expressed concern about his anti medication bias and one senior psychiatric hospital administrator said that while not agreeing with him it is important to hear other views. While defending the rights of people to present their opinions, I am concerned that Dr. Fisher gives the wrong message and that can be dangerous. Much of what he talks about is "touchy feely" unscientific new age platitudes combined with some common sense and a message that serious mental illness is not physiological.

How often have we heard someone with severe depression being told to "snap out of it"? Asking the question or expecting the depressed individual to cure their own depression implies that it is not a disease but a personal failure. You can't "snap out of" a broken leg or an occluded blood vessel. But, Dr. Fisher seems to think that you can overcome what he calls a severe emotional distress (SED) that is precipitated by trauma or loss. When an individual suffers this SED, they often are taken over by the mental health system and labeled as severely mentally ill.

He further discounts the medical model by stating "the present mental health care system is based on an illness model in which an expert defines the problem as primarily a defective chemical mechanism in the patient's brain that needs to be repaired by the expert. This model reduces symptoms but interferes with the person's taking an active role in recovery." In that same paper, he states "all of us can achieve self control of symptoms to varying degrees...." And "genuine healing comes from within by an activation of our own healing powers".

This is from a paper he had published in 1994 in "Hospital and Community Psychiatry" that he handed out at his workshop as if we have not made numerous advances in the past 10 years. First, serious mental illness is just that – an illness of the brain. One needs to look at the many imaging studies of the brains of people having a first episode psychosis compared to normal controls to realize that.

Dr. Fuller Torrey has an excellent paper in which he reviews 65 studies of individuals with schizophrenia who had never been treated with medications that indicate significant abnormalities in brain structure.

How can you achieve self-control of symptoms when the symptoms are caused by circumstances beyond your control like abnormalities of the brain? You can't. That is like telling someone with epilepsy that they can will away their seizures.

These notions are the same as those in cancer where it is suggested that you can control your cancer and its spread through imaging, visualization, laughter, prayer, biofeedback, and other similar modalities. I could not find any studies in the medical literature that support this. A few years ago, I did an article on group therapy and its ability to help ameliorate the symptoms of advanced cancer and help to prolong life.

I did a group interview with women who were dying of advanced metastatic breast cancer but who were part of a study to see if group support might help their symptoms and prolong life. All of the women expressed intense dislike for the proponents of the visualization treatment. They all said that the implication is that their failure to control their cancer and get better is their fault. It is not. They were very ill and they were going to die and it was not because they did not want to live or they were not visualizing hard enough. But, the consequence of this New Age concept of will your way to better health is to demean their suffering and their incredible strength.

The same goes for serious mental illnesses like schizophrenia. Dr. Fisher may not need medication for whatever reason but most do. When I asked him why people experience a return of symptoms when they go off medication, he said that it might be because they were not far enough along in their recovery process. What balderdash! What does that mean?

I can give him all sorts of examples as most can of the return of symptoms that are so bad that people have committed suicide as a consequence. But, here is an example of someone who was recovered. A man with schizophrenia who took his medication, worked full time at a career, was married and was enjoying his retirement and his many hobbies. The doctors decreased his anti-psychotics and his symptoms came back and he had to be hospitalized until the increased dosage kicked in.

I'm not sure how Dr. Fisher would account for that but I think of the comments made in a presentation by Dr. Robert Zipursky who was head of the Centre for Addiction and Mental Health in Toronto and is now head of psychiatric services in Hamilton, Ontario. Dr. Zipursky said about 80% of patients will relapse within the first five years if they stop taking their medications. But, even if they are in remission, they should stay on indefinitely because of the cumulative damage each psychotic episode inflicts. "Recovery from relapse may take a long time and it is uncertain," he said. Scientists, he added, still don't know if someone can remain well for five or 10 years without medication, and the risk of not recovering from a relapse is too great. "If you've spent a year or two getting someone well and watching them rebuild their lives . . . to watch them get sick again is not something you would wish on anyone,"

Are these people much different than Scientologists?

Alternative Medicine

Regardless of the disease, there are those who advocate against medical science for what they believe are safer and more natural remedies. But there really is no such thing as alternative medicine. According to the paper "From Alternative Medicine -- The risks of untested and unregulated remedies" in the New England Journal of Medicine 339:839-841, 1998 by Marcia Angell and J Kassirer we have "There cannot be two kinds of medicine -- conventional and alternative. There is only medicine that has been adequately tested and medicine that has not, medicine that works and medicine that may or may not work.

Once a treatment has been tested rigorously, it no longer matters whether it was considered alternative at the outset. If it is found to be reasonably safe and effective, it will be accepted. But assertions, speculation, and testimonials do not substitute for evidence."

If something is proven to work then it works but unfortunately no vitamin concoction or herbal preparation has been definitely shown to be effective in schizophrenia. There was some suggestion that vitamin B3 might be effective in some instances but that is controversial and not thoroughly tested. No vitamin or herbal product is of any value for schizophrenia or bipolar disorder and yet many people want to take something that they think might be safer.

Nothing is safe when given in large doses and many vitamins and herbal products can be toxic, have negative side effects and/or interact with prescription drugs. Ginkgo biloba prolongs bleeding time so adds to the effect of drugs like coumadin and aspirin and can be dangerous. St John's Wort interacts with many drugs and reduces the effectiveness of anti-retrovirals used for HIV, birth control pills and cyclosporin used to prevent rejection in the case of transplants.

There is no magic bullet when it comes to the treatment of schizophrenia or any other serious mental illness like bipolar. We desperately need to find something that works better than what we presently have.

But it should also be pointed out that psychiatric medicines have about the same efficacy, and the same numbers and kinds of side effects as the current medicines available for chronic medical illness like heart disease, MS, HIV, arthritis, diabetes. The difference in outcomes may be in the partnership between the patient and the health care provider.

There are psychiatric patients who completely refuse medications. Then, there are those who are ambivalent or reluctant. This latter group takes their medications some of the time but will not or cannot work with the doctor to find the most effective medicine with the least side effects. Thus only about 25 percent of people with schizophrenia actually engage with the doctor to find and adjust medication over time as someone with say diabetes might do. If they actually did or could (which might be not possible given that the very organ needed for cooperative insightful partnerships is impaired) the treatment results could be much better.

CHAPTER NINE – CREATIVITY, MENTAL ILLNESS AND FAMOUS PEOPLE WITH SCHIZOPHRENIA

K ay Redfield Jamison has an excellent book called "Touched with Fire" [103] that deals with the relationship between art and madness. Most of the book deals with bipolar disorder and is interesting reading. Because of diagnostic confusion between bipolar disorder and schizophrenia, many artists who were once thought to be schizophrenic such as Ruskin, Schumann, Strindberg, Woolf, Pound, Poe, Artaud, Dadd and van Gogh would not be so diagnosed today.

Jamison comments on P 74 of her book that people with schizophrenia are less likely to be creative given the disorganizing and dementing characteristics of the disease. According to the schizophrenia dot com website, "there are relatively few famous people with schizophrenia because schizophrenia is a brain disorder that typically strikes people when they are quite young - age 17 to 28. People this age typically are too young to be famous, they are just starting out their professional lives after completing high school or college."

The information for this section comes from that website

That site does have an extensive list of notable people with schizophrenia or who have relatives with the disease. Some of them were mentioned in the section on genetics. James Joyce had a daughter with schizophrenia. Bertrand Russell had an uncle and both a son and a granddaughter with the disease. Einstein also had a son with schizophrenia. Alan

Alda's mother as well. It is suspected that Abraham Lincoln's wife might have had schizophrenia.

Of course, the best known is John Nash, the subject of the very popular film, "A Beautiful Mind", and a Nobel prize winning mathematician. Others include:

Tom Harrell a jazz musician who has been called the John Nash of jazz. Against considerable odds, Harrell has successfully struggled with schizophrenia and become one of the most respected trumpeters and composers of the past 30 years.

Meera Popkin was the star of "Cats" and "Miss Saigon" on Broadway and in London's West End and was diagnosed with schizophrenia during this time. Her life went from center stage and limousines to waiting tables at Wendy's, but she's now back and is doing well.

Andy Goram - Scottish Soccer Player/Goal Keeper - It has been reported in the UK Newspapers that Scottish goalkeeper Andy Goram who playing for Rangers and as a sub with the Manchester United FC Soccer club was diagnosed with schizophrenia. Goram is regarded as Scotland's top goalkeeper and among the best in Europe despite the knee injuries which have dogged him throughout his Rangers career. His superb reaction saves and bravery have earned him World Cup recognition since earning his first Scotland cap while an Oldham Athletic player in 1986.

Lionel Aldridge Superbowl-winning Football Player

Peter Green of the band Fleetwood Mac

Syd Barrett of the band Pink Floyd

Alexander "Skip" Spence and Bob Mosley - both members of the 1960's rock group Moby Grape (and Jefferson Airplane for Skip Spence)

Roger Kynard "Roky" Erickson of the Austin-based 1960's group The Thirteenth Floor Elevators. Around 1967 Erickson was arrested for drug possession and locked in a psychiatric hospital for schizophrenia. When Erickson came out of the psychiatric hospital (1972), he published a book of poetry. Despite his mental instability, he hit the scene again during the rush of psychedelic revival and punk-rock, with dark humor and a taste for the supernatural that carried him away from his origins, towards a macabre rhythm and blues.

Joe Meek - 1960's British record producer ("Telstar"). From 1960 until his premature death six years later, Joe Meek released 245 singles, 45 of which made the Top 50.

James Beck Gordon (Jim Gordon) - James Beck Gordon had been, quite simply, one of the greatest drummers of his time. In the Sixties and Seventies he had played with John Lennon, George Harrison, Eric Clapton, the Everly Brothers, the Beach Boys, Judy Collins, Joe Cocker, Frank Zappa, Duane Allman, Carly Simon, Jackson Browne and Joan Baez. But the music came to an end as he developed schizophrenia.

Charles "Buddy" Bolden - BBC News [104] reported that the mental health problems of one musician could have led to the creation of jazz. Without his schizophrenia, Charles "Buddy" Bolden - the man credited by some with starting off the jazz movement - might never have started improvisation.

Vaclav Nijinsky The famous Russian Dancer whose career ended after World War I when he developed schizophrenia.

AFTERWARD

As was stated in the introduction, schizophrenia is a very debilitating disease both for the victims and for their families. The amount of research into the disease has increased in the past few years but, as you saw, we are a long way from unraveling its mysteries. A more concerted effort needs to be made and that will only come about when society recognizes the physical causes of the problem and when the stigma associated with it is defeated.

Much greater emphasis is needed to educate society in order to improve understanding. Improved understanding of psychiatric disorders first began with depression when some celebrities who suffered from this problem began to openly talk about their illness. This then expanded to other conditions such as obsessive compulsive disorder and even bipolar disorder. It is only just now reaching schizophrenia but we need to make a much greater effort to reduce the stigma associated with this disease.

We also need to recognize signs of potential schizophrenia in young people when they first begin to appear. This is not easy, as you saw, but it is crucial. Increased understanding and early intervention might just possibly lead to better compliance on the part of the ill. With greater understanding of the nature of the disease, will come an increased awareness that by working with their physicians the ill will be able to find an appropriate medication and dose that will help them improve.

163

REFERENCES

1. World Health Organization "Schizophrenia" at
   http://www.who.int/mental_health/topics.html
2. World Health Organization Regional Office for
   Europe, Press Release, EURO/01/05 at
   http://www.euro.who.int/mediacentre/PR/2005/20050
   110_1/
3. World Health Organization Regional Office for
   Europe, Press Note, EURO/15/04 at
   http://www.euro.who.int/mediacentre/Conference/20
   070307_1?

4. "De-Criminalizing Mental Illness", M.J. Stephey,
   Time Magazine, August 8, 2007
5. Symposium: Mentally Ill Defendants in Jail, Friday
   April 13, 2007, UM School of Law
6. Statement of Judge Steve Leifman before the
   Subcommittee on Crime, Terrorism and Homeland
   Security of the Committee on the Judiciary of the
   United States House of Representatives concerning
   "Criminal Justice Responses to Offenders with
   Mental Illness", March 27, 2007
7. Mary Beth Pfeiffer, Crazy in America, New York,
   Carroll and Graf Publishers, 2007
8. E. Fuller Torey, Out of the Shadows, New York, John
   Wiley and Sons, 1997

9. "Jailing the Mentally Ill: It Harms Them, Harms Other
   Inmates and is Very Costly" from the Eagle Tribune
   newspaper and posted on
   http://www.schizophrenia.com June 4, 2007
10. "Mentally Ill need treatment not jail, report says" from
    the capitalnewsonlineat
    http://www.carleton.ca/jmc/enews/18112005/n3print.
    shtml

11. "Number of prisoners with mental illness on upswing: rreport", from CBC news Nov 4, 2005 at http://www.cbc.ca/story/canada/national/2005/11/04
12. "Calls to get mentally ill out of jails" Simon Kearney and Adam Cresswell, The Australian, July 16, 2005
13. "Visionary Leader Needed For Mental Health Advocacy Position" job ad posted on http://www.schizophrenia.com on Aug 3, 2007
14. "Homeless suffering more mental illness", August 7, 2006 and posted on http://www.monstersandcritics.com
15. "Mental disorders account for more than half of hospital stays among the homeless in Canada", August 30, 2007, Press Release from the Canadian Institute for Health Information
16. "Homeless Shelters are de facto Mental Institutions", October 20, 2005 news blog report from Australia at http://www.schizophrenia.com
17. "Homelessness among people with severe mental illness in Switzerland", Christoph Lauber et al in Swiss Med Weekly 2005,135:50-56
18. "Decade of the Brain" at http://www.loc.gov/loc/brain/proclaim.html
19. "Mental Health: A Report by the Surgeon General at http://www.surgeongeneral.gov/library/mentalhealth/chapter1/sec1.html
20. President's New Freedom Commission on Mental Health at http://www.mentalhealthcommission.gov/
21. "Nation's Mental Healthcare system gets "D" Grade, March 1, 2006 on http://www.NAMI.org
22. "Mental Health Implementation Task Force Reports, Ministry of Health and Long Term Care, Ontario at http://www.health.gov.on.ca/english/providers/pub/m hitf/mhitf_mn.html

23. Speech by Michael Wilson in Oakville Ont, Oct 2003 and reported on by Marvin Ross for the Business Executive news paper
24. "Out of the Shadows at last" The Standing Senate Committee on Social Affairs, Science and Technology, Ottawa, May 2006, chaired by The Hon Michael J. L. Kirby
25. Green Paper "Improving the mental health of the population: Towards a strategy on mental health for the European Union, Health and Consumer Protection Directorate General, Brussels 2005
26. "Crying Shame of Stigma, The Priory Group, UK, August, 2007 at http://www.priorygroup.com/pg.asp?p=home
27. Saha, S et al "A systematic review of mortality in schizophrenia: is the differential mortality gap worsening over time?" Arch Gen Psychiatry 64(10) 2007
28. Newcomer JW, Hennekins CH "Severe mental illness and risk of cardiovascular disease, JAMA 2007; 298:1794-1796
29. Seeman Mary V "An outcome measure in schizophrenia mortality, the Canadian Journal of Psychiatry vol 52 no 1 Janualry 2007
30. "A secret life of madness", John M Glionna, LA Times, Sept 10, 2007
31. biography of Fred Frese on the NAMI website at http://www.nami.org
32. "A schizophrenic offers insider's view of illness", Marvin Ross, The Medical Post, May 4, 1999
33. Interview with Ian Chovil
34. From the http://www.chovil.com website
35. Interview and correspondence with the author
36. Nancy C Andreason, Brave New Brain, Oxford University Press, 2001

37. Abram Hoffer, Adventures in Psychiatry, The Scientific Memoirs of Dr. Abram Hoffer, Kos Publishing, Caledon, Ont., 2006
38. PRIME Clinic website at http://www.med.yale.edu/psych/clinics/prime/services.html
39. http://www.schizophrenia.com/schizpictures.html
40. New Imaging Research Reveals dysfunction in the Brain's "Hub" in the Earliest Stages of Schizophrenia", Jan 1, 2001, Science Daily on http://www.sciencedaily.com
41. "hallucinations in Schizophrenia Linked to Brain Area that Processed Voices, August 1, 2007, Science Daily on http://www.sciencedaily.com
42. E. Fuller Torrey, "Studies of Individuals with Schizophrenia Never treated with Antipsychotic Medications: A Review" and posted on http://www.psychlaws.org
43. Gur, RE et al, "Deconstructing Psychosis with human brain imaging", Schizophr Bull, 2007 Jul; 33(4):921-931
44. Freedman, R "Neuronal Dysfunction and Schizophrenia Symptoms" Am J Psychiatry 164:385-390, March 2007Symposium
45. Tsuang, M "Schizophrenia: Genes and Environment, Biol Psychiatry, 2000 Feb 1;47(3):210-220
46. McGuffin P "Nature and Nurture Interplay: Schizophrenia Psychiatric Prax 2004 Nov;31 Suppl 2 S189-93
47. Expert Interview with Nancy C Andreason on Medscape "Shcizophrenia and Neuroimaging: http://www.medscape.com
48. Yolken, RH and Torrey, "Infectious Agents in Schizophrenia and Bipolar Disorder, Psychiatric Times, June 2006 Vol XXIII no. 7

49. Torry, EF et al, "Antibodies to Taxoplasma gondii in Patients with Schizophrenia: A Meta-analysis, Schizophrenia Bulletin, doi:10,1093/scbul/sb1050

50. Schweiler, L et al, "Increased levels of kynurenic acid in the central nervous system may account for neuropsychiatric symptoms in patients with tick borne encephalitis, a paper presented at the Neuroscience 2007 conference in San Diego on Nov 5, 2007

51. Zammit, S et al, "Self reported cannabis use as a risk for schizophrenia in Swedish conscripts of 1969: historical cohort study" BMJ 2002:325:1199 (23 November)

52. Semple DM et al, "Cannabis as a risk factor for psychosis; systematic review" J Psychopharmacol 2005 March; 19(2):187-94

53. From Wikipedia

54. Seeman, P "Schizophrenia: An Essay by Dr. Philip Seeman, Nov 2001 in special topics on http://www.esi-topics.com

55. Expert Interview, "Probing the biology of psychosis, schizophrneia and antipsychotics: An Expert Interview with Dr. Philip Seeman" on Medscape at http://www.medscape.com

56. Ross, Marvin Report on Glycine on http://www.schizophrenia.com

57. Dugan, L et al, "How ketamine (special K) impairs brain circuitry" study from the UC San diego released Dec 3, 2007 press release and published in the Dec 7 Journal Science

58. The Scientist, Dec, 2007 special supplement on schizophrenia and available at http://www.the-scientist.com/supplement/2007-12-1/

59. "Nutrients cure Mental Illness" on http://www.newmediaexplorer.org/sepp/2005/11/07/n

utrients_cure_mental_illness_orthomolecular_psychi
atry.htm

60. Lerner, V "Treatment of Acute Schizophrenia with Vitamin Therapy", study registered with clinicaltrial.gov

61. Torrey, E and Judy Miller, The Invisible Plague, The Rise of Mental Illness from 1750 to the Present, Rutgers University Press, 2001

62. Interview with Fuller Torrey on the Rutgers Press website

63. Accordino, MP, "Deisnstitutionalization of Persons with Severe Mental Illness: Context and Consequences" Journal of Rehabilitation, April-June 2001

64. "WHO expresses urgent need for network of community care" on theschizophrenia.com news blog posted June 6, 2007 from the Global Forum for Community Mental Health held in Geneva May30-31, 2007

65. "Anosognosia keeps patients from relaizing they're ill" from the Psychiatric News, Sept 7, 2001, vol 36 No 17, p 13

66. "Violence real issue for untreated brain disorders" from the Treatment Advocacy Center website at http://www.treatmentadvocacycenter.org/

67. Diane Rehm National Public Radio Show broadcast on April 25, 2007 after the Virginia Tech shootings. A discussion with Torrey, Thomas Insel, Director of the NIMH and David Shern, president of Mental Health America.

68. Bailey, S "Man hailed by some as genius cannot be forcibly drugged for metal illness, June 6, 2003, Canadian Press news story

69. "How the mentally ill are treated in Norway", posted on schizophrenia.dot news blog on October 5, 2005,135:5

70. Mental Health Services in Norway, Prevention Treatment Care, Norwegian Ministry of Health and Social Services, publication number I-1025E
71. Psychiatric Hospidtals (Compulsory Admissions) Act Status as of June 2004, International Publications Series Health Welfare and Sport no. 4, The Hague, June 2004, Ministry of Health Welfare and Sport
72. Mental Health Act 2007, brief summary of provisions in the Mental Health Bill, Newsletter number 14 of the Royal College of Psychiatrist, UK
73. Consensus Guidelines, Canadian Psychiatric Association, at http://ww1.cpa-apc.org:8080/Publications/Clinical_Guidelines/schizophrenia/november2005/index.asp
74. Consensus Guidelines, American Psychiatric Association at http://www.psych.org/psych_pract/treatg/pg/SchizPG-Complete-Feb04.pdf
75. CPA Guidelines written for lay public at http://www.schizophrenia.ca/mysql/CPAGuidelinesFinalE.pdf
76. Interview with Professor McGorry, Australian Broadcasting Corporation, Four Corners April 3, 2005
77. "Latest research indicates early intervention in schizophrenia key to improving outcome, NAMI press release April 22, 1997
78. Report on early detection and intervention for young people, National Institute for Mental Health in England and on their website at http://www.nimhe.csip.org.uk/
79. From the Coalition For Appropriate Care and Treatment website at http://www.cfact.ca
80. O'Reilly, R "Why are community treatment orders controversial?" Can J Psychiatry 2004;48:579-584

81. Hunt, AM et al, "Community treatment orders in Toronto: the emerging data" Can J Psychiatry vol 52 no 10 Oct 2007

82. Jenkins, Chris L, "Va studies directives giving the mentally ill a say in their care", The Washington Post, Sept 10, 2007

83. Psychiatrist in Blue website at http://www.pmhl.ca/en/index.html

84. "The Sherriff as Advocate" in Catalyst Treatment Advocacy Center Feb 2007

85. Heslop, L et al, "Trends in Police Contact with Persons with Serious Mental Illness in London, Ont", Consortium for Applied Research and Evaluation in Mental Health, Research Update, Autumn 2002, University of Western Ontario Lawson Health Research Unit

86. In Germany, approximately 30% of people with schizophrenia able to work" posted on the schizophrenia.com news blog Dec 4, 2007

87. Pijl, VJ et al, "Change in dutch mental health care: an evaluation" Soc Psychiatry Epidemiol 2000 35:402-407

88. Schene AH, et al, "Mental health care reform in the Netherlands" Acta Psychiatr Scand 2001:104 (Suppl 410) 74-81

89. Personal attendance at Billy Crystal performance at the Canon Theatre in Toronto

90. Priest, D and Anne Hull, "A Soldier's Officer" Washington Post Dec 2, 2007

91. Storring, Russell, "86 years for a pardon" CBC News Analysis and Viewpoint Nov 5, 2004 on CBC.ca/news

92. Gillan, Audrey, "Jailing of Iraq veteran raises questions about combat stress" the Guardian, April 11, 2006

93. Stuart, H et al "Community Attitudes toward people with Schizophrenia" in Can J Psychiatry 2001;46:245-252
94. "Doctors are prejudiced against patients with mental health disorders" June 23, 2007 report on Medical News Today reporting on the RCP conference
95. Hamilton Spectator, July 20, 2002
96. Davidson, G "Inquest is a good idea" letter to the Amilton Spectator Jusy 23, 2002
97. Shuchman, M "Separate mental illness from other symptoms", Globe and Mail Sept 3, 2002
98. "Tom Cruise officially criticized, Hubbard had schizophrenia" schizophrenia.com news blog Sept 6, 2005
99. Mieszkowski, K "Scientology's war on psychiatry" Spiegel online July1, 2005
100.   "Germany moves to ban scientology" BBC News, Dec 8, 2007
101.   Satel, S. PC MD How Political Correctness is Corrupting Medicine, 2000, Basic Books
102.   Ross, Marvin "Editorial a review of a Dan Fisher workshop" on schizophrenia.com May 27, 2005
103.   Jamison, Kay Redfield, Touched with Fire, New York, Free Press, 1993
104.   "Mental illness at the root of jazz" BBC News, July 10, 2001

ALPHABETIC INDEX

700 Sundays..137

A Beautiful Mind.. 160
acetylcholine 94
ACT.. 126
adrenaline 96
adrenochrome... 94,95
adrenolutin 97
agonist 86
Alabama... 35
Alberta.. 146
Alda, Alan 162
Aldridge, Lionel.. 160
Allman, Duanne 161
alogia 58
Amador 107
American Journal of Psychiatry 69
American Psychiatric Association (APA)............... 53, 88, 98, 120
American Psychological..33
amino acid 86, 95
AMPA... 91
Ampakines 91
amygdala...67, 68
Andreason, Nancy 11, 51, 74, 138
angel dust (PCP) 80, 86
Angell, Marcia 156
anhedonia 58
anosognosia 58, 107
Arboleda-Florez, Julio.. 145
Archives of General Psychiatry 28
Arkansas.. 16
Artaud, Antonin 159
 ascorbate...100
atypical antipsychotics... 85
auditory cortex 72
Australia 19, 22, 28, 125, 132
Australian Broadcasting Corporation 123
B3...96, 156
Baez, Joan 161

173

Baltimore..21, 76
Barrett, Syd..160
Basal ganglia 59, 70
Beach Boys..161
Bijlani, Natasha..143, 148
Biological Psychiatry..87
Bleuler, Eugen..57
Bolden, Charles "Buddy"..161
bovine disease viruses 76
Braitmen, Ken..18
 Breggin, P.R..61
Brian's Law..109
British Columbia..96
Broca's motor speech area..71
Brown, Joyce..113, 119
Browne, Jackson..161
Bureau of Research in Neurology and Psychiatry............................96
Bush, George..23
California..17
Campaign for Abolition of the Schizophrenia Label 55
Canada 18, 22, 122, 131, 146
Canadian Forces 141
Canadian Institute for Health Information....................................22
Canadian Journal of Psychiatry..29, 146
Canadian Mental Health Association....................................19, 147
Canadian National Committee for Police/Mental Health Liaison................131
Canadian Psychiatric Association 120
Canadian Senate..27
cannabis..81
Capgras syndrome 47
Carrey, Jim 139
Catalyst..132
Cats..76, 160
CBS TV..139
Centre for Addiction and Mental Health..155
cerebral cortex..70
cerebrospinal fluid..62, 68, 75, 86
Chevy Chase..76
chickenpox..78
chlorpromazine 82, 85, 101, 145
cholinergic system 94
Chovil, Ian 19, 37
chromosome..79
Citizens Commission on Human Rights 150

Clapton, Eric 161
Cleveland Plain Dealer 105
Cleveland State Hospital 102
Clozapine 85, 88, 92, 122
CMV 79
Coalition for Appropriate Care and Treatment (CFACT) 126
Cocker, Joe 162
Cognitive and Negative Symptoms in Schizophrenia Trial (CONSIST) 88
Collins, Judy 161
Columbia University 106
community treatment orders (CTOs) 128
congressional committee 17
Connecticut 24, 117
consumer survivor 12
corpus callosum 68
Crazy in America 16
Cruise, Tom 149
Crying Shame 143
   Crystal, Billy 137
CSF 68, 79
CT scans 61, 62
CTOs 129
CX516 92
Cytomegalovirus (CMV) 79
d-cycloserine 88
D-serine 86, 91
D2 receptors 84
Dadd, Richard 159
Dallaire, Romeo 141
Davidson, Gwen 148
Decade of the Brain 23
deinstitutionalization 20, 28, 30, 32, 82, 104, 122, 128, 134
Demonologie 52
Department of Justice 111
Descartes, Rene 51
Detroit 66
DNA elements 79
dopamine 60, 69, 84
Dr. Phil 139
Duckworth, Ken 26
Dudek, Kenneth 104
Dyskinesias 63
dyspraxia 64
Early Psychosis Prevention and Intervention Centre (EPPIC) 124

175

Edgar Eager Lodge...22
Edinburgh High Risk Study...68
EEG 66
Egyptian Ebers Papyrus 52
eidomics...74
Einstein, Albert...75, 159
electric or insulin shock..82
endogenous retroviruses 79
England..27, 125, 143
epilepsy...51
Erickson, Roger Kynard "Roky" 161
Eslinger, Donald F. 132
Europe 32
European Union..27
Everly Brothers 161
extrapyramidal 63
factor M...96
Fisher, Daniel...152, 155
Fitzpatrick, Michael J 140
Florida 35, 132
Florida Atlantic University 29
Foundation of Patient Councils (LPR) 135
Fountain House 104
France..133
Freedman, Robert...70
Frese, Fred 35
Freud, Sigmund 53
Freudians..52, 54
frontal cortex...70
Frontal Lobe..59
Frontline 16
frontotemporal...68
functional magnetic resonance imaging (fMRI 67
Galen 50, 52
Genetic polymorphisms 77
genomics 72
Germany 134
glial cells 69
glutamate 91
glutamatergic system..85
Glutamic acid 86
glycine...86, 92
glycine transporter – 1 90
GlyT-1 90

Goff, Donald C 91
Goram, Andy..160
Gordon, James Beck (Jim) 159
graphesthesia 64
Gray, John P..53
Greece 27
Green, Peter 160
Guelph 37, 39
haldol 80, 82, 85,130
hallucinogens...96
haloperidol 82
Hamilton..36, 147, 152, 155
Hamilton Spectator 148
Hammer of Witches 52
Harrell, Tom 160
Harrison, George 161
Harvard 91
Harvard Law School. 114
Harvard Medical School..73
Harvey, William..50
Health Care Consent Act 116
Hennekens, Charles H...29
Heresco-Levy, Uriel 87
Herpes simplex viruses..78
herpes virus 80
hippocampus 60, 78
Hippocrates..52
Hoffer, Abram 54, 95, 98, 100
Homewood Health Centre 37
Hospital and Community Psychiatry...154
HSV-1 78
HSV-2 78
HSV-3 78
Hubbard, L. Ron 150
Illinois...25
influenza 76
Institute of Medicine of the National Academy of Sciences..............23
Institute of Psychiatry...60
Iraq war 141
Italy, ...134
Jaffe, D. J...113
Jamison, Kay Redfield 159
Japanese 55
Javitt, Daniel 88

JC Chasez 139
Jefferson Airplane 161
Johns Hopkins University School of Medicine 76
Joint Resolution 174 23
Journal of Rehabilitation 104
Journal of the American Medical Association 29
Joyce, James 75, 159
Kaplan, Seymour 105
Karolinska Institute 80
Kassirer, Jerome 156
Keener Men's Shelter 20
Kendra's Law 109, 129
ketamine 80, 86, 93
Koch, Ed 114
Kraeplin 65
Krebs cycle 97
kynurenic acid (KYNA) 80
LA Times 34, 117
Laing, R.D. 54
Langsley, Donald 105
lateral ventricles 62
Lauer, Matt 149
League of Clients 135
Leiberman, Jeffrey 106
Leifman, Steve 15
Lennon, John 161
Limbic System 60
Lincoln, Abe 160
Lippman, Robert 114
Lithuania 27
lobotomies 82
London 132
long-term potentiation, or LTP 91
Los Angeles 60
LSD 95
MacArthur Foundation 111
Mad in America 61
magnetic resonance imaging 60
magnetic resonance spectroscopy 69
Maine 24
Malleus Maleficarum 52
Malone, Darren 146
Manhattan Spirit 113
Manhattan State Hospital 20, 83

Marrett, Penny 19
Maryland 35, 76
Massachusetts 21
McGill 83
McGlashan, Thomas 117
McGorry, Patrick 123, 125
McGrath, John 28
Me Myself and Irene 139
medial temporal lobe 68
Meek, Joe 161
Melbourne 124
Mental Health Act 116
Mental Health Act 2007 118
Mescaline 95
Mill, John Stuart 128, 129
Miss Saigon 160
Mitchell, Alex 146
Moby Grape 161
Montreal 83
Moonves, Leslie 140
Mosley, Bob 161
MOT 128
MRI 60
muscarinic acid 94
myoclonic 63
N-acetyl-aspartate 69
N-methyl-d-aspartate 85
N'Sync 139
NAA 69
NAD 97
NADPH oxidase 93
NAMI 18, 24, 26, 35, 122, 138
Nash, John 160
National Coalition of Human Rights Activists 150
National Committee for Mental Hygiene 53
National Empowerment Center 152
National Institute for Mental Illness 125
National Public Radio 113
National Reform Movement 103
NBC Today 149
negative symptoms 57, 69, 86
Neolithic times 51
Netherlands 119, 133
Neuroscience 2007 80

179

Neurotransmitters 60, 69, 84, 86
neurotropic...78
New England Journal of Medicine 156
New Hampshire 18
New Jersey Psychiatric Institute...96
New South Wales 19
New York 20, 104, 107 129
New York City 83
New York Civil Liberties Union 114
New York State Psychiatric Institute...106
Newcomer, John...29
niacin...95, 98
niacinamide..92, 95, 98, 100
nicotinamide adenine dinucleotide (NAD) 97
nicotinic receptor..94
Nijinsky, Vaclav..162
NMDA 86, 90, 93
noradrenaline 97
North Carolina...129
Norway...117, 118
Nova Scotia 38
O'Reilly, Richard 129
Occipital Lobe 60
Ohio 20, 24, 35, 74, 104
olanzapine 87,89
On Liberty 128
Ontario..26, 36, 109, 115, 126, 127 147, 152
Ontario Consent and Capacity Board 115
Ontario Superior Court..116
Oprah...139
orthomolecular psychiatry 95, 98
Osmond, Humphrey...95,100
oocytes...76
Ottawa...109
Out of the Shadows 20
Out of the Shadows at Last 27
Oxford...33
P.C. MD 151
Pandora 135
PANSS..91
parasite 76
parasthesias 65
Parkinsonian 63
parkinsonism symptoms 83

patient confidential counselor (PVP) 135
PBS.. 16
PCP.. 86
PET 69
Pfeiffer, Mary Beth 16
phenomics 74
Phil Donahue Show 114
Piotrowski, James.. 142
Plato... 51
pneumoencephalography 62
Poe, Edgar Allan.. 159
Popkin Meera... 160
positive symptoms 57, 69, 85
positron emission tomography (PET) 67
Potter, Rusty.. 147
Pound, Ezra.. 159
prefrontal cortex... 80
premorbid... 89
PRIME clinic 56, 89, 123
Princeton.. 96
Priory Group 143
Priory Hospital 27
prodromal 89, 121, 123
prodrome 56
proteomics 74
Psychiatric Times... 75
psychoanalysis 53
pyridoxine 100
Queensland Centre for Mental Health Research 28
quetiapine 85
Regina 96
Rehm, Diane.. 113
Rice, David 150
Rikers Island 16
risperidone 87, 91, 101
 Rockefeller University...83
Roehampton 143
Royal College of Psychiatrists 146
rubella 76
Ruskin, John... 159
Russell, Bertrand 73, 159
Rwanda... 141
Sacrasine.. 90
Saks, Elyn.. 33

San Diego 80
San Francisco 21, 30, 34
SANS 91
Saskatchewan 95
Satel, Sally 151
Schizophrenia: The Sacred Symbol of
Psychiatry 54
Schizophrenia Bulletin 67
Schizophrenia Research 87
Schizophrenia Society of Canada 120
Schizophrenia Society of Ontario 19
Schumann, Robert 159
Schutzman, Scott Jeffrey 115
Science 93
Scientific American 75
Scientist 133
Scientologists 149, 156
Scotland 68
Seeman, Mary and Phillip 29, 83
Seminole County 132
septal region 67
serotonin 85, 90
Sharma, Tonmoy 61
Shields, Brooke 149
Shuchman, Miriam 148
Siebert, Al 151
Simon, Carley 161
single photon emission computed tomography (SPECT) 67
sleep spindles 71
South Carolina 24
South Florida Evaluation and Treatment Center 15
SPECT 69
Spence, Alexander "Skip" 161
SSRI anti-depressants 90
St. Joseph's Health Centre 147
Stanley Laboratory of Developmental Neurovirology 76
Stanley Medical Research Institute 76
Starson, "Professor" 115
Starson case 115
State University of New York at Buffalo 148
stigma 137, 144
stigmabusters 138
Stockholm 80
Strindberg, August 159

Stuart, Heather 145
superoxide 93
Supreme Court of Canada.. 115
Surgeon General of the United States.. 23
Switzerland 22
Sydney.. 22
synapses.. 84, 86
syphilis 80
Szasz, Thomas... 54
T. gondii. 76, 77, 80
tardive diskinesia (TD)... 63, 83
temporal lobe 69
Texas 35
thalamic reticular nucleus 71
thalamus 60, 65, 68
The Center Cannot Hold.. 33
The Center for Mental Health Services 151
The Invisible Plague 101
The New Asylums... 16
The Snake Pit 102
The Thirteenth Floor Elevators 161
The Time is Now... 26
Tick borne encephalitis (TBE) 80
Time Magazine 15, 17
Toronto... 39, 86, 88,130, 155
Toronto Globe and Mail 148
Torrey, E. Fuller...................... 20, 21, 27, 40, 52, 61, 75, 101, 104, 113, 154
Touched with Fire 159
Toxic Psychiatry... 61
toxoplasma 77
Toxoplasmosis.. 78
transcranial magnetic stimulation 82
Treatment Advocacy Center... 20, 116, 132
trephined... 51
Tsai, Guoschuan.. 90
typical antipsychotics... 82, 84
UK... 21, 55, 118, 133
UN.. 141
University of Alabama... 96
University of California San Diego 93
University of Edinburgh... 67
University of Minnesota 95
University of Pennsylvania, ... 67
University of Southern California 33

University of Toronto..29, 83, 148
US...22, 28, 31, 36, 51, 53, 122
US Marines 36
USC 35
valacyclovir 79
van Gogh 159
varicella zoster virus 78
Vermont 17
Victoria 96
Virginia Tech..113
vitamin B3 95
Walter Reed Army Hospital 141
Washington Post..130, 141
Washington University 29
Wayne State University 67
Wernicke's area..60
Wernicke's receptive speech area...71
Western Reserve Psychiatric Hospital 36
Whitaker, Robert...61
Whiteside, Elizabeth 141
Wilson, Michael..26
Wisconsin 24, 35, 126
Woods, Scott W 89
Woolf, Virginia..159
World Health Organization...14, 106
Wyoming 17
Yale...33, 56, 89, 117
Yale University..89
Yolken, Robert H 75
Ypsilon 135
Zappa, Frank 161
Zipursky, Robert 155
zyprexa 130

ABOUT THE AUTHOR

Marvin Ross is a medical writer/journalist in Dundas, Ontario, Canada. This is his eleventh book - four are on health topics for the lay public. Including this one, they are: "The Silent Epidemic: A Comprehensive Guide to Alzheimer's Disease", "Eyes" which was endorsed by both the Canadian Medical Association and the Canadian Association of Optometrists and "Pig Pills Inc: The Anatomy of an Academic and Alternative Health Fraud".

His writings have appeared in numerous medical and lay publications and websites. He wrote a regular column for Schizophrenia Digest and writes for the website schizophrenia dot com. As a journalist, he has attended and written about both the Canadian Psychiatric Association and the American Psychiatric Association annual conferences.

Marvin is past president of the Hamilton chapter of the Schizophrenia Society of Ontario and was on the Ontario board. He was also on the executive of the Hamilton Program for Schizophrenia Family Association and the steering committee for the Hamilton Talking About Mental Illness Program. He is presently involved with the Coalition for Appropriate Care and Treatment in Ontario.

In 2006, he was appointed by the Government of Ontario as a public member to the College of Opticians of Ontario. One of the College's main roles is protection of the public. He is a member of the executive and sits on the quality assurance and patient relations committees.

ABOUT DAVID DAWSON

Formerly Professor of Psychiatry, McMaster University, and Psychiatrist-in-Chief at Hamilton Psychiatric Hospital, Dr. Dawson now works part-time in clinical psychiatry, primarily with families, children, and adolescents. He devotes the rest of his time to teaching, writing, film making, and painting. He is the author of two academic books:

He has also written five novels and several screenplays. His film credits include "Manic", "My Name is Walter James Cross", and "Drummer Boy".

His films and novels usually contain mental health themes, including schizophrenia, bipolar disorder, Alzheimer's, and addictions. And there is a relationship between his interest in Borderline Personality Disorder and his literary endeavours: There are many times, in our attempts to understand human behaviour, when we need to bypass medical and psychological models, and think instead in the manner of a novelist or playwright.

Novels

Last Rights St. Martin's Press, New York, N.Y., 1990. Macmillan of Canada, Toronto, 1990. Also translated and published in Denmark, Iceland, Holland, Germany, England, Norway, Sweden, France, and reprinted in paperback, New York

Double Blind St. Martin's Press, New York, N.Y., 1992 Macmillan of Canada, Same European Publishers as above

Essondale Macmillan of Canada, Toronto, 1993. Same European Publishers as above

The Intern Macmillan of Canada, March, 1996, (ILLUSTRATED BY AUTHOR)

Non Fiction Books

Schizophrenia in Focus Human Sciences Press, New York, 1984

Relationship Management Taylor & Francis, New York, 1993

Plays, Screenplays, Film, Video

Whose Mind Is This Anyway? 50 minute one act play, written, directed and produced by David Dawson, 1989

Who Cares David Dawson and Alex Chapple, 40 minute dramatic video, 1990

Manic Written by David Dawson, directed by Alex Chapple, one hour dramatic film, made for **TV Ontario, 1993**

The Waiting Room, one half hour 1 act play, written, directed, produced by David Laing Dawson for International Gerontology Conference, 1994

My Name is Walter James Cross, One hour drama, filmed in BetaCam, written and directed by David Dawson, First Window broadcast by **TV Ontario, 2001,** distributed by **Films for the Humanities and Sciences.**

The Three Harolds, Screenplay for theatre optioned by pat ferns productions

I Swear to God, Screenplay for theatre (suspense/thriller with female lead),

Stray Dogs, Screenplay for theatre

The Good Buy, Screenplay for theatre

Painting with Tom, David and Emily, DVideo Production, short, DVD, 15 minutes, 2005, written, directed, edited by David Laing Dawson

Cutting for Stone, 96 minute drama, Written and Directed by David Dawson, Filmed in DVCPRO50, Post Production completed December 2007

Breinigsville, PA USA
20 January 2011
253775BV00003B/56/P

9 780981 003702